BASIC COLLEGE WRITING

SECOND EDITION

BASIC COLLEGE WRITING

SECOND EDITION

Laurie G. Kirszner
Philadelphia College of Pharmacy and Science

Stephen R. Mandell
Drexel University

W · W · Norton & Company · New York · London

Library of Congress Cataloging in Publication Data
Kirszner, Laurie G.
  Basic college writing.

  Includes index.
  1. English language—Rhetoric. I. Mandell, Stephen R. II. Title.
PE1408.K674   1981   808'.042   81–11017
ISBN 0–393–95180–4   AACR2

W. W. Norton & Company, Inc. 500 Fifth Avenue, New York, N.Y. 10110
W. W. Norton & Company Ltd. 37 Great Russell Street, London, W.C. 1

1 2 3 4 5 6 7 8 9 0

Contents

Preface   xi

To the Student   xiii

Section I — Essay Structure   *1*

Chapter 1 — The Whole Essay   *3*

The General Structure   *3*

The Parts   *5*

1. The Introduction   *5*
2. The Body Paragraphs   *6*
3. The Conclusion   7

The Whole Essay   *8*

Examples   *13*

1. A Lab Report   *13*
2. A Midterm Examination   *14*
3. A Letter of Application   *16*

Chapter 2 — From Topic to Controlling Idea   *24*

Limiting and Angling Your Topic   *25*

Considering Your Boundaries   *26*

1. Length   *26*
2. Purpose   *26*
3. Audience   *27*
4. Occasion   *27*
5. Knowledge   *28*

Deciding What to Write About   *29*

1. Listing   *29*
2. Brainstorming   *30*

The Controlling Idea   *34*

  1. The Narrow Controlling Idea   *34*
  2. The Broad Controlling Idea   *35*

Chapter 3 — Structuring Your Essay   *40*

  The Narrow Controlling Idea   *40*

  The Broad Controlling Idea   *44*

  Common Structuring Patterns   *56*

  1. Illustration   *56*
  2. Comparison-Contrast   *57*
  3. Cause and Effect   *59*
  4. Classification and Division   *60*
  5. Process   *61*

Chapter 4 — Revising Your Essay   *65*

Section II — The Paragraphs   *71*

Chapter 5 — The Introductory Paragraph   *73*

  What It Does   *73*

  1. Attracting Attention   *73*
  2. Holding Attention   *74*
  3. Stating the Controlling Idea   *74*

  Some Examples   *75*

  1. Direct Announcement   *76*
  2. Quotation or Dialogue   *78*
  3. Anecdote   *79*
  4. Definition   *81*
  5. Refutation   *82*
  6. Series of Unrelated Facts   *84*
  7. Question   *86*

  Choosing an Appropriate Introduction   *89*

Chapter 6 — The Body Paragraphs   *96*

Structure of the Body Paragraphs   *96*

1. The Topic Sentence   *96*
2. Placement of the Topic Sentence   *100*
3. Development   *106*
4. Transition   *110*

How the Body Paragraphs Work in the Essay *113*

Chapter 7 — The Concluding Paragraph   *122*

What It Does   *122*
Some Examples   *125*

1. Restatement   *125*
2. Chronological Wind-up   *126*
3. Illustration   *127*
4. Prediction   *128*
5. Recommendation of a Course of Action   *130*
6. Quotation or Dialogue   *131*

Choosing the Best Conclusion   *132*

Chapter 8 — Revising Your Paragraphs   *138*

Section III — The Sentences   *143*

Chapter 9 — Sentence Patterns   *145*

Defining the Sentence   *145*

The Patterns   *145*

1. The Simple Sentence   *145*
2. The Compound Sentence   *150*
3. The Complex Sentence   *151*
4. The Compound-Complex Sentence   *154*

Using Sentence Patterns   *156*

Chapter 10 — Sentence Style   *160*

Sentence Economy   *160*

1. Deadwood   *160*
2. Redundancy   *161*

Sentence Variety   *166*

1. What Is Sentence Variety?   *166*
2. Revising to Achieve Sentence Variety   *169*

Chapter 11 — Incorrect Sentence Patterns   *173*

The Sentence Fragment   *173*

Run-on Sentences   *176*

Misplaced Words or Phrases   *181*

1. Misplaced Modifier   *182*
2. Dangling Modifier   *185*

Faulty Parallelism   *186*

Shifting Perspectives   *191*

1. Shift from Past to Present Tense   *191*
2. Shift from Active to Passive Voice   *191*
3. Shift from Singular to Plural   *191*
4. Shift from First Person to Third Person   *192*
5. Shift from Statement to Question   *192*

Agreement Errors   *194*

1. Subject-Verb Agreement   *194*
2. Pronoun-Antecedent Agreement   *197*

Section IV — The Words   *201*

Chapter 12 — Choosing the Right Word, Part I   *203*

Overused Words   *203*

1. Substituting a Pronoun   *203*
2. Substituting a Synonymous Word
   or Expression   *204*

Inexact Words   *205*

    1. Confusing Two Words   *205*
    2. Commonly Confused Word Pairs   *207*
    3. Blending Two Expressions   *212*

Idioms   *214*

Levels of Usage   *217*

    1. Slang   *217*
    2. Colloquial Style   *218*
    3. Formal Style   *218*
    4. Informal Style   *219*

Chapter 13 — Choosing the Right Word, Part II   *222*

    Choosing Specific Words   *222*
    Choosing Original Words   *225*
    Choosing Effective Words   *227*
        1. Connotation and Denotation   *227*
        2. Slanting   *233*

Chapter 14 — Revising Your Sentences and Words   *236*

Appendix — A Combined Checklist   *241*

    Organization   *241*
    The Paragraphs   *241*
    Sentences and Words   *241*

Index   *242*

Preface

Our aim in the first edition of *Basic College Writing* was to help students learn to write competently at the college level and to enable them to gain a command of organization and style that would also serve them well after they left college. In this second edition our goal is the same.

We know from experience that most beginning writers find it useful to learn a single general-purpose plan of organization and to learn that one thoroughly. The plan we teach is the thesis-and-support paper, which lends itself to a variety of uses for the college student: from "themes" to essay-question answers to job-application letters. Its requirements of the writer are clear-cut; most students can, therefore, understand teacher evaluations and become good self-critics.

In this second edition we remain convinced of the value of this organization plan and of its ability to provide students with skill and confidence. We are even more convinced of this structure's flexibility and its adaptability to a wide range of academic assignments. For this reason, we have been careful in this edition to clarify our emphasis on students' actual writing and reading in academic situations and to stress the concept of writing as a skill that can be applied to tasks in all subject areas.

In this edition we have also added more material on the writing process, including an expanded discussion of prewriting in Chapter 2 and additional material on revision in Chapter 4. In Chapter 3, we have added a new discussion of common structuring patterns (illustration, comparison-contrast, cause and effect, classification and division, and process). We have added a detailed treatment in Section II on the placement of the topic sentence. In Section III we have supplied more information on·punctuation; on when to use simple, compound, and complex sentences; and on agreement errors. Finally, in Section IV, we take up commonly confused word pairs, among other things. Throughout, we have relied on those who used the book to tell us what worked and what didn't, and we have incorporated their suggestions into this revision. Thanks to their advice, a good many examples and exercises are new to this edition, and key explanations have been expanded and polished. The result, we think, is a better book, more useful to students and to teachers.

We owe a lot to a great many people. John Francis's insightful and thorough assessment of the first edition's strengths and weaknesses gave this edition direction and made the process of revision orderly and efficient. We remain, as always, awed by his critical skills. In the final stage of our revisions, helpful constructive criticism from Harry Brent of Rutgers University, Camden, Tom Waldrep of the University of South Carolina, and Michael Cronin of Oklahoma State University enabled us to put the finishing touches on the manuscript. We are grateful to Barry Wade at Norton, who took up where John Francis left off, for helping us to get the final draft in shape. We are also grateful to Helen Falls, who typed the manuscript with a speed and an accuracy that spoiled us forever. And, when we looked up between chapters, Demi and Mark (and David and Adam and Rebecca) were still there. For that, we are most grateful of all.

To the Student

Contrary to popular opinion, a knowledge of how to write well is not something that comes naturally. It's a skill that most people have to work to develop. This book tries to aid in your development as a writer by helping you to master the basic form of most college writing: the 350-to-500-word essay.

Basic College Writing is divided into four sections. The first section is about the general structure of the short essay. It develops a schematic model or diagram that illustrates that structure and gives you a pattern for organizing your ideas into an essay. The second section of the book examines the paragraphs in the essay, and discusses the different techniques and patterns that work in introductory, body, and concluding paragraphs. The third and fourth sections deal respectively with the sentences and the words of the essay. Here we focus on the many varieties of sentence structure and word choice available to you as a writer.

The emphasis of this book is upon writing not simply for your English courses, but for *all* your subjects. It gives you a tool, a method, a step-by-step approach that works for all the kinds of writing you will do in college. You can use this method for writing essay exams, lab reports, term papers, business letters, and much else. As you will see, all these kinds of writing are variations of the short essay form; if you can write a coherent, well-organized and developed 350-500-word essay, you will be able to write at the college level.

ESSAY STRUCTURE

Section I presents a general idea of what an essay is and how it is structured. We offer a simple, straightforward method for organizing and writing a short essay—a method that should remove the mystery and difficulty many students associate with college writing. Chapter 1 is an overview of the whole essay. In Chapter 2, we discuss how to choose a topic, narrow and angle the topic by considering the essay's boundaries, find material to write about, and decide on a controlling idea. In Chapter 3, we show how to structure an entire essay using its controlling idea. Finally, in Chapter 4, we present a series of revisions that will help you in revising your own essays.

CHAPTER 1

The
Whole Essay

The General Structure

It seems logical that before you try to put a jigsaw puzzle together you should have a good idea what the shape of the finished product will be. This is also true when it comes to writing an essay. Before you spend time writing and revising, you should decide what it is you are trying to create.

Just about all essays have three basic parts:

Introduction

Body

Conclusion

In college writing the standard short essay is between 350 and 500 words long. This usually means that your essay will have a one-paragraph introduction, a three-paragraph body, and a one-paragraph conclusion:

Title

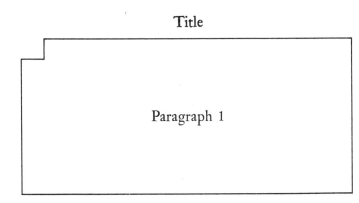

Introduction

Paragraph 1

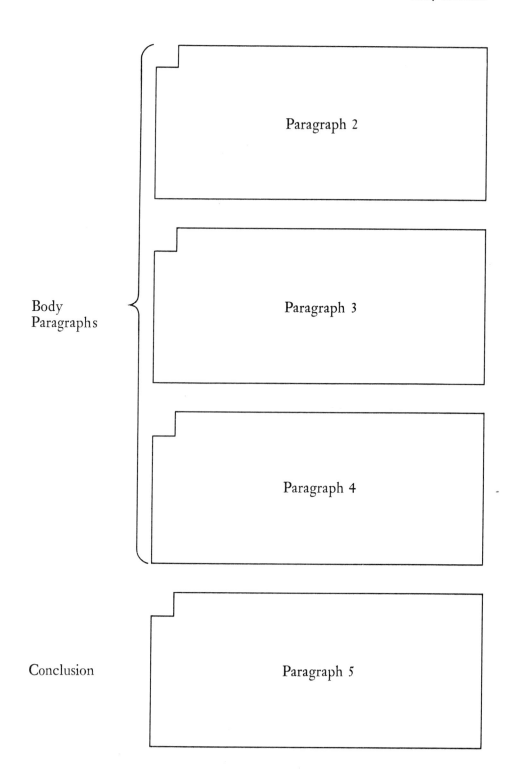

Body
Paragraphs

Paragraph 2

Paragraph 3

Paragraph 4

Conclusion

Paragraph 5

Of course, not every writing assignment you have will conform exactly to this pattern. On the whole, however, the principles in this chapter can be applied to all the writing you do in college.

The Parts

1. The Introduction   The introduction is the first section of your essay. This makes it extremely important, because first impressions are often lasting ones. Your introduction should be interesting to your readers. If it is dull and matter-of-fact, the chances are it will turn them off, and they will not read further. Besides stimulating your readers' interest, your introduction has a structural purpose: it should state the essay's main idea or thesis statement. This statement is called the *controlling idea*. This controlling idea is what tells your readers what the essay they are reading will be about. Without a clearly stated controlling idea, your essay will seem to be just a loose collection of unrelated statements. The controlling idea brings your essay into *focus*, giving it direction and drawing its ideas together. Usually put at the end of your introduction, the controlling idea is the central element of your essay, because it indicates what points you will discuss in detail in the body of your essay.

Generally, the introduction to a short essay is a full paragraph, not just a single sentence. It usually begins with remarks designed to interest your readers. As it progresses, your introduction should present general facts or ideas that will orient your readers to your essay's subject. As it proceeds further, your introduction should gradually narrow its focus, and move from introductory remarks to controlling idea smoothly and logically. The "shape" of your introductory paragraph should look something like this:

Introduction

General introductory remarks _____

_____ → controlling idea.

Keep in mind that the purpose of your introduction is to arouse interest and introduce your controlling idea, *not* to present a full discussion of your topic. Development of the major points of your essay is the job of the next section of your essay, the body paragraphs.

2. The Body Paragraphs   The body paragraphs are the longest single section of your essay. In a short essay, there are usually three body paragraphs, each one considering in detail one aspect of the essay's controlling idea. This is called a *three-point essay*. At the beginning of each of your support paragraphs, there is usually a *topic sentence* that tells what the rest of your paragraph is going to be about. This topic sentence should direct your readers back to the controlling idea and indicate which aspect of it you are going to discuss in your paragraph. Your topic sentences should be as specific as the controlling idea. Just as your controlling idea provides a focus for your essay, your topic sentences provide a focus for your body paragraphs.

Once your topic sentence presents the point to be discussed in the body paragraph, you need details and facts to *support* it. It is not enough to state your position; the people reading your essay need to be convinced that your position is valid or that your impressions are accurate. It is your job, not your readers', to show the logic of your argument.

There is no hard and fast rule that determines how long a body paragraph should be. The more relevant detail you can bring in to support each of your topic sentences, the clearer your points will be. If your points are well stated and adequately supported, your essay will be solid and convincing. Most of the time each of your body paragraphs will resemble the following diagram:

Body
Paragraph

Topic sentence _____

_____→ supporting detail
(examples, reasons, or arguments).

3. The Conclusion Because it ends your essay, the conclusion stays with your readers the longest. Therefore, the ideas in your conclusion must be consistent with the rest of your essay.

In your conclusion, you should draw together all that has come before by restating your controlling idea. This restatement is usually most effective when it is located at the beginning of your conclusion. Not only does this repetition remind your readers of the major points you have been trying to make, but it also signals them that your essay is drawing to a close. An abrupt conclusion, or one that does not follow logically from what has come before it, can jolt your readers and raise doubts about the entire essay. It is therefore helpful to follow your restatement of the controlling idea with some general concluding remarks. These statements should gradually widen the focus of the controlling idea and have the effect of easing your readers out of the essay and back into *their* world. Many writers like to end their conclusions with a final emphatic statement. This strong closing statement will cause your readers to think about the implications of your essay.

None of the material mentioned in the conclusion should contradict or change your controlling idea. Apologies or disclaimers will only undercut your essay's arguments. For the same reason, you should not introduce any entirely new points in your conclusion. New points require new proof; you don't want to reopen the discussion just when you were trying to conclude it. In general, the shape of your conclusion should look like this:

Conclusion

Restatement of controlling idea _____
_____→ general
concluding remarks _____
_____→ final statement.

Remember that each of your essays should have an introduction, body paragraphs, and a conclusion. After you finish the first draft of your essay, check to make sure that each section does its job. Also, make sure your essay is balanced. You should not have an introduction or conclusion that is excessively long or short. Finally, make sure that your essay has a descriptive title. This title should not only catch your reader's eye, but also give your audience a clear idea of what your essay will be about.

EXERCISE 1

Just to check your understanding of the concepts, define the following terms in your own words:
1. Controlling idea
2. Topic sentences
3. Body paragraphs
4. Focus
5. Support
6. Three-point essay

The Whole Essay

Because all parts of your essay are based on it in one way or another, your controlling idea is especially important: your introduction states it, each of your body paragraphs discusses one aspect of it, and your conclusion restates it. The following diagram shows how all parts of your essay work together.

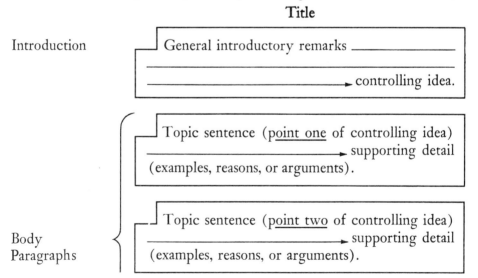

Title

Introduction

> General introductory remarks _____
> _____ ► controlling idea.

Body Paragraphs

> Topic sentence (point one of controlling idea)
> _____ ► supporting detail (examples, reasons, or arguments).

> Topic sentence (point two of controlling idea)
> _____ ► supporting detail (examples, reasons, or arguments).

Topic sentence (point three of controlling idea) → supporting detail (examples, reasons, or arguments).

Conclusion

Restatement of controlling idea ⎯⎯⎯ → general concluding remarks ⎯⎯⎯ ⎯⎯⎯ → final statement.

The following paper by Michael Shay, written for a composition class, conforms to the above model. In his essay, Shay explores the possible long-range effects of unrestricted technology. It is clear that he is familiar with the principles we have discussed. He knows, for instance, that his essay should have an introduction, several body paragraphs, and a conclusion. He also understands how each part of his essay works and how the controlling idea functions in his essay.

Title

And on the Last Day Man Created . . . .

Introductory Remarks

Should man play God? The question is no longer just a subject for philosophy and metaphysics. To-day's technology offers us the potential to change ourselves and our world in ways we never dreamed of before. Perhaps a more appropriate question is at what point in the realization of our potential do we begin to destroy ourselves? Should we continue to allow the unrestricted proliferation of tech-nology? And when do we begin to consider more carefully the full consequences of our actions? Three recent developments illustrate the dangers that lie ahead of us and suggest that we may have already become the guinea pigs of our own tech-nology.

Controlling Idea

Topic
Sentence

The current problems with nuclear power plants represent one potential danger technology holds for us. During the past six months seven nuclear reactors automatically shut down due to malfunctions in their cooling systems. The danger here is that a malfunction may be so serious that even an automatic shutdown would be too late or that the shutdown itself would not work in an emergency. The accident at Three Mile Island in 1979 started with a seemingly insignificant event, the failure of a pump. A series of operator actions, equipment failures, and design defects caused what should have been a minor problem to balloon into the most serious accident ever to befall a nuclear power plant. Fortunately, no one was killed, but experts agree that it was largely a matter of luck that a massive core meltdown did not occur, resulting in the contamination of much of central Pennsylvania.

Topic
Sentence

Genetic engineering presents another example of the dangers of uncontrolled technology. Researchers at Princeton and Stanford Universities have been able to recombine sections of DNA strands, the material that defines the hereditary characteristics of an organism, to form sequences never before known. Consequently, when this type of work is being done, there is always a question of just what will be synthesized. Eminent scientists have speculated on the possibility of creating dangerous life forms, which, because of their uniqueness, could not be controlled by medical efforts. Despite the safeguards instituted in laboratories engaged in DNA experimentation, many researchers worry about new bacterial forms escaping into the environment.

Topic
Sentence

The dumping of chemical wastes is a final danger of unrestricted technology. Chemical wastes are the by-products of our highly industrialized society. Effluence from factories, refineries, and waste treatment plants is piling up faster than we can economically dispose of it. Many of these chemicals are highly toxic or carcinogenic and must be stored in metal drums before they can be disposed of in areas called chemical dumps. The Environmental Protection Agency estimates that of the 50,000 chemical waste dumps in the United States, 2000 may pose serious health hazards. Experts familiar with this situation have called these dumps "chemical time bombs." They worry that if enforceable laws that place limits on chemical dumping are not enacted soon, a catastrophe of unimaginable proportions could occur.

Restatement

Concluding Remarks

We cannot be blind to the dangers our modern technological society presents to all of us. The long-term consequences of our way of living are, as yet, still unknown. Nevertheless, recent occurrences indicate that we are rapidly approaching a point of no return. Before it is too late we should assess the cost of our advanced technology both to ourselves and to our environment. Only then will we be able to make the difficult decisions necessary to get us safely through the next decade.

Shay begins his essay by asking a series of questions calculated to draw his readers into his essay. He structures his essay around his controlling idea that there are three examples that illustrate the dangers of modern technology. In each of his body paragraphs he goes on to discuss one of these examples in detail. Notice that Shay moves easily from one illustration to another by including clear transitions in his topic sentences: "The current problems . . . represent *one* . . . danger"; "Genetic engineering presents *another* [danger]"; and "The dumping of chemical wastes is a *final* danger." In his conclusion, Shay restates his controlling idea, then gradually widens his focus, and ends with a strong closing statement.

EXERCISE 2   The following essay was written in a composition class on the topic "Write Your Own Obituary." Because of the special demands of this topic, it does not conform exactly to the diagram. Nevertheless, even in the case of an unconventional topic like this, the resemblance is striking. To clarify that resemblance, underline the controlling idea in the introduction; then underline the topic sentences in the four body paragraphs. Finally, underline the restatement of the controlling idea in the conclusion.

Title

Andrew Laurence Dies in Los Angeles

Introduction

Andrew (Bull) Laurence, well-known scientist, professional football player, community activist, and family man, passed away last evening; the cause is unknown. Scientists are working around the clock trying to pinpoint the cause of his death. Laurence's fellow scientists believe his death to be a result of the "Mars Bacteria" which threatened the world back in 1987, but nothing is certain at this time.

Laurence won the Nobel Prize for his excellence in science in 1998. His vaccine for the "Mars Bacteria" was the basis for the synthetic vaccine used today in the fight against Martian Pox. Laurence gave credit for his great success in science to his alma mater, the California College of Intergalactic Research.

Recognized not only for his contributions to science, Laurence was also one of the best running backs in the game of professional football. Powering through lines, breaking tackles, and literally running over his opponents, Laurence led his team to three national championships. His retirement from the pros was a big letdown for his team, the L.A. Rams, as well as for his many fans.

Body
Paragraphs

Laurence loved the game of football, but he had an even stronger love for the children who followed the game. Sunday afternoons, you could find "the Bull" in the park, playing ball with the kids, or at one of the clinics he set up to keep kids off the street. Laurence was also involved in such community activities as judging science fairs, arranging the annual Junior Science Award Dinner, and setting up a fund-raising project to refinish the town statue of Emilio Avogadro.

Despite his considerable achievements in the areas of science, sports, and community service, the most important part of this great man's life was his family. His wife, Michele, will continue to reside in the family home in San Jose, Calif. Laurence's daughter, Cindy, a nuclear physicist, is married to Dr. Michael Cone. They live in Denver, Colo., with their daughter, Amy. Scott "Moose" Laurence, "the Bull's" son, who played at U.S.C. and furthered his career with the Dallas Cowboys, is now an NBC sportscaster.

Conclusion

Kelley's Funeral Home will have services for Andrew Laurence on Wednesday and Thursday from 2 to 5 P.M. and 7 to 9 P.M. It is expected that notables from the worlds of science and sports will join with members of the community and Laurence's family to honor a truly great man and to mourn his passing.

Examples

1. **A Lab Report**   The essay pattern we have been discussing applies not just to the essays you write in English class. Another area in which you might find this essay pattern helpful is in explaining a scientific process. Precision, exactness of expression, and objectivity are particularly important in scientific research. In the following write-up of an experiment, notice how direct the controlling idea is and how extremely clear and straightforward the topic sentences are.

The Destructive Distillation of Wood

The destructive distillation of wood, the first experiment assigned this semester, involves the observation of an organic substance, wood, as it breaks down into its components. When the vapor given off by the wood is cooled, wood alcohol (CH_3OH) can be obtained. <u>This experiment consists of three basic steps.</u>

<u>Gathering equipment is the first step.</u> For this experiment you need two eight-inch test tubes, a beaker, ice, a rubber hose, two small one-holed rubber stoppers, a Bunsen burner, and some wood. (Three or four wood chips are enough.)

<u>The next step in the destructive distillation of wood is setting up the experiment.</u> Begin by placing one test tube in a beaker filled with ice, and then put the wood chips in the other test tube. When the ends of the rubber hose are placed in the holes of the stoppers and the stoppers are put in the test tubes, both test tubes are connected to the hose. The Bunsen burner is then held under the test tube containing wood.

<u>From this point on, the experiment proceeds quickly; in fact, the third and final step consists simply of watching the results.</u> First, vapor begins to rise from the wood and goes through the hose to the other test tube. When the vapor is cooled by the ice, it becomes a liquid. This procedure continues for about five minutes, until all the wood has turned black. At this time, the test tube in the beaker contains liquid wood alcohol (CH_3OH) and acetic acid (CH_3COOH) and gaseous carbon monoxide (CO) and carbon dioxide (CO_2). The first test tube contains the wood residue, which is a black substance called charcoal. Thus, the destructive distillation of wood produces a complex mixture of solids, liquids, and gases that could be recovered by fractional distillation if desired.

<u>The basic steps in the destructive distillation of wood are relatively easy to perform, and the results are easily observed.</u> Therefore, this experiment serves as a good introduction to basic laboratory techniques as well as to some of the fundamental principles of distillation.

2. **A Midterm Examination** You can also use this essay pattern in your midterms and final exams. A stu-

dent's midterm, reproduced below, answered the question "What do you think the concept of freedom meant to Andrew Marvell and Henry David Thoreau?" Since the student, Judy Konrad, was asked to discuss two writers, her essay has two body paragraphs. If she had more material about the two writers, she might have decided to spend *two* paragraphs discussing each, for a total of *four* body paragraphs. In either case, the pattern for the essay is the same: introduction, body, conclusion. The controlling idea of this essay has been underlined. Underline the topic sentences and the restatement of the controlling idea.

Freedom and Time

Time is a dimension that embraces everyone and is controlled by none. The most anyone can do is to control himself and "budget" time, but in today's complicated world people constantly complain they "have no time." "Time flies." It "runs out." And at the same time, people complain of a lack of freedom. To many, including Henry David Thoreau and Andrew Marvell, this freedom could only come with a release from the burden called time.

Thoreau feels we must simplify, thereby saving time and becoming free. He himself left the pressures of society to live in the woods and see if he could learn what life had to teach. In his new environment he discovered how to live, how to find the freedom he lacked, and how to gain more time, and he expressed it all for society in "Why I Went to the Woods." Here he speaks of all the useless things men waste time on: "Our life is frittered away by detail"; "We are determined to be starved before we are hungry"; "In eternity there is indeed something true and sublime. But all these times and places and occasions are now and here." These are a few of the ways he expresses himself.

Andrew Marvell expresses the whole concept of time as freedom beautifully. In his poem, "To His

Coy Mistress," a man is trying to convince a woman
that they lack the time to go through the entire
courtship ritual. He feels the passage of time and
says so: "Had we but world enough, and time,/This
coyness, lady, were no crime." He continues, exag-
gerating, and tells her that at the rate at which she
is progressing, her beauty will soon fade and the
worms will be feasting on her decaying virgin flesh.
Again he states his concern about time: "But at my
back I always hear/Time's winged chariot hurry-
ing near." As a finale, he again repeats his message
that they must hurry to make the most out of life
and live for the moment: "Thus, though we cannot
make our sun/Stand still, yet we will make him run."

Both Thoreau and Marvell express their concern
over a lack of time. They seem to say that this lack
puts pressure on us and makes us feel less free. How
many people are preoccupied with detail and trivia?
These are people who might feel trapped by society
and who could gain freedom by simplifying and al-
lowing more time for simple yet important things.

In the first paragraph, the student introduces the
central idea she will be discussing: freedom equals release from the limits of time. The last sentence of her
first paragraph states her controlling idea.

In the second paragraph she shows, by referring to
one of his writings, how Thoreau expressed his need
for freedom; in paragraph three she relates her concept
of freedom to Marvell's "To His Coy Mistress."

In her final paragraph, she restates her main point:
both writers feel constrained by a lack of time. She
goes on to extend this concept, applying it not just to
two writers, but to society in general.

3. **A Letter of Application**   The essay pattern is used
not only in student writing, but in much business or
technical writing too. A standard letter of application
for a job also depends for its effect upon a controlling
idea, topic sentences, and a restatement of the control-

ling idea. Underline these elements as they appear in the following letter. Notice how they aid the applicant by reinforcing his qualifications.

243 Ludlow Avenue
Cincinnati, Ohio 45220
April 15, 1982

Mr. H. Yankovich
Upsala Chemical Research Inc.
2106 Montgomery Road
Cincinnati, Ohio 45236

Dear Mr. Yankovich:

I am writing in response to the ad you placed in the Sunday paper for a part-time laboratory assistant. Next year I will receive a Bachelor's degree in chemistry, and this job would give me the experience I would need for my future career in this field. I believe that both my education and experience are directly related to your needs.

As an undergraduate I have taken many courses in chemistry. I have developed a great deal of practical expertise, and can, at this point, perform most laboratory procedures with little or no difficulty. Because my primary interest is in polymer chemistry, I feel assured that I could carry out any assignments you would give me.

Besides taking courses, I have done other work in chemistry. During the past two years at the University, I have been working in the laboratory storerooms of the chemistry department. In addition, I spent last summer helping Dr. H. Hanikah do research in quantum chemistry.

I would welcome the opportunity to join your staff because your company enjoys a reputation for helping students such as me to gain experience in industry. I am enclosing a résumé and could be available for an interview at your convenience.

Sincerely yours,
ADAM BECK

EXERCISE 3 Longer pieces, such as term papers and magazine or journal articles, may also follow the essay pattern. In each of the following two essays, underline the controlling idea, the topic sentences, and the restatement of the controlling idea. Notice that "Why We Still Can't Wait," a *Newsweek* editorial by Coretta Scott King, while longer than the previous examples, still has a five-paragraph structure. The second essay, a short paper discussing several different aspects of the American character, differs from our model in that it has more than three body paragraphs.

Why We Still Can't Wait †

Twelve years ago when my husband, Martin Luther King, Jr., sat in the Birmingham jail during the civil-rights campaign in that city, he received a letter from a group of concerned white clergymen. While they recognized the clear justice of his cause, they wondered would it not be better to ask for less and accept that one must wait for progress. My husband's answer, written on scraps of paper and smuggled out of his cell, was one of the great documents of the civil-rights movement. The "letter from a Birmingham jail" laid out for all Americans the moral and social reasons why we can't "wait." I was reminded of Martin and the letter from a Birmingham jail recently when I went to Washington to testify in favor of the "Humphrey-Hawkins Full Employment and Balanced Growth Act of 1976"—a measure that would commit the government to take all practical steps to lower unemployment to 3 per cent for adults by 1980. Although the issue was different, full employment rather than civil rights, and involved both black and white Americans, once again the less fortunate were being told that practical men had decided for them that it would be better to "wait." My husband can no longer raise his voice in reply, but there is no question what his answer would be. There are three burning reasons why America's jobless cannot wait for some far-off day before we have full employment.

The first reason is that our current high unemployment is nothing less than a guarantee that America's future will hold deterioration rather than progress. The men and women breadwinners of America are not isolated individuals but a pivot on which the whole health of our community depends. A man with a decent job is a provider for his children and a model for their behavior. He is the support of his aging parents and a force for stability in his neighborhood and city. Clean and safe streets, decent housing, adequate medical care and even racial peace are all goals that can only come from a base of stable jobs. Without decent jobs, neither the "special programs" of the cautious nor the pious lectures of the uncaring can do anything but add the insult of indifference to the injury of unemployment. Nothing less than the future of America is at stake. Right now a new generation is growing up, all too many in homes where the parent is without work. Tolerating high unemployment in 1980 will be nothing less than a guarantee that we shall walk down dirty streets, past bitter youths and sad-eyed old men, on into the 21st century. High unemployment is nothing less than a vile investment in continuing decay.

The second reason why America's unemployed cannot wait is that the last 30 years have offered compelling proof that waiting is no solution at all. Do we really need to be reminded that the many postwar cycles of prosperity and recession have always left millions of Americans behind? Have we forgotten that in 1968, when the deceptive unemployment rate was below 4 per cent, the ghettos of America were in flames? Millions of people involuntarily work part-time or shuffle from one poverty-level job to another, all of them excluded from the unemployment rate we watch so closely. Genuine full employment requires a major improvement of our educational system and expanded job training to prepare the unemployed for good jobs. It requires tax and regulatory policies to ensure that jobs are located where people can reach them, and not policies that encourage the "export" of jobs to foreign countries. It requires not "leaf raking" but major investment in mass transit, in energy and a host of projects that will benefit all America. And not a single one of these things will be achieved by waiting. Full employment will be achieved by forceful government action or it will not be achieved. The proposal that we wait is in reality the proposal that we do nothing.

The final and most compelling reason why America's unemployed cannot be told to wait is that full employment is at base a moral issue, and questions of justice cannot be solved by waiting. We who support full employment know full well that there are realistic limits to our economic capacity and we do not ask for miracles. All we seek is an America where every person is given the chance to productively contribute to his country and where he can receive a fair and equitable share of the wealth that production creates. There is no economic mystery in this; only a simple demand for justice. The current government policy, on the other hand, is deeply unfair. Accepting unemployment to control inflation amounts to choosing the people at the very bottom of the economic pyramid to bear the entire economic burden. In the so-called war against inflation, America's 10 million unemployed have been made the Administration's conscript army.

Yet, there are those who try to avoid this moral issue. Full employment is indeed a just and decent goal, they say, but it is just too complex to be solved with a clear and direct government commitment to its elimination. To be frank, I cannot but consider this the most reprehensible evasion of all. Since when have we begun to decide our ethics on the basis of how difficult they are to fulfill? In 1963 we did not decide our view of the Civil Rights Act on the basis of whether it would create complex problems of litigation. What we asked was whether God created all men equal. In 1965 we did not ask how much the Voting Rights Act would cost in terms of Federal inspections. We asked if America was indeed to be a land of justice and a country of free men. And so today what we must ask is not whether full employment will be simple or convenient or cheap, but whether tolerating unemployment is morally right or wrong. For myself, if the alternative to full employment is simply to wait, to tolerate in silence the shattered dreams of jobless youth and the broken hearts of laid-off old men, then my choice is clear. America's jobless cannot "wait," not only because waiting is no solution and not only because waiting has social consequences that are frightening to contemplate, but because to do nothing when we have the capacity to act is morally and socially wrong.

The Unique Species

Americans are unique; there is no other nation on earth so peculiar as ours. Our tastes, our hobbies, our habits, our likes and dislikes—our very nature makes us unique. From the first moment we draw breath we are clearly a part of a strange and distinct nation.

We Americans are lazy. We spend most of our time trying to avoid effort or work. We begin our day by driving to work instead of walking. We ride elevators to our jobs instead of climbing stairs. Throughout the day, those of us who are homemakers use a multitude of time-saving appliances such as electric mixers, blenders, and sweepers to keep ourselves from doing our own work. When not doing "work" like operating an automatic washer or dryer, we Americans can usually be found using telephones instead of visiting or writing letters, or watching television instead of reading or entertaining ourselves. When our day is over, we can usually be found turning to a frozen meal—or a restaurant—for our dinner.

We Americans use too many machines. We wake up to the sound of an alarm clock, a machine. We cook our breakfast on the stove, a machine. We travel in cars, trains, trolleys, and planes, all machines. We use machines in all of our occupations. The farmers among us use tractors, combines, and reapers; office workers use typewriters, computers, and calculators, all machines. We Americans don't use our hands any more, because we have too many machines.

We Americans eat too much junk food, which is low in nutritional value and full of worthless calories. We buy these junk foods at supermarkets; what cannot be purchased there is found at fast-food restaurants or in vending machines. Americans eat junk food at the movies, and while watching television. And we don't eat junk food just for snacks—we substitute it for our main meals. The capacity of Americans to consume junk food is evident in the extremely high sales of food like Fritos, potato chips, Cokes, Swanson TV dinners, Big Macs, Heroburgers, doughnuts, and Hershey bars.

We Americans are sports nuts. We are seen, almost every weekend, rushing madly to the stadiums, wolfing down hot dogs and popcorn during every excitement-filled moment. If we aren't dashing to the stadium, we are sitting in front of the television set watching the game. But we Americans do not just watch sports, we play them too.

We are out in the fields and streets and schoolyards of America playing unorganized baseball games, mismatched softball games, and lopsided basketball games. Our amateur sports events are really free-for-all social gatherings, unlike the big business-controlled professional sports.

We Americans love violence, and sports like football, hockey, and wrestling are not the only areas in which violence is glamourized. Our media are full of violence. Newspapers and magazines are dominated by articles on crime, riots, and war. Such publications as *Detective* and *True Confessions* highlight people's misfortunes, portraying them as victims of crime and acts of God. The types of television shows most frequently seen substantiate this interest in violence: westerns and detective shows full of shooting, and the aforementioned sports programs.

We Americans are too interested in sex. Half the average American's day is spent listening to sex propaganda. We turn on our televisions to relax and the first thing we see is a toothpaste commercial asking, "How's your love life?" If television commercials don't fill up our sexual void, we head for the nearest adult bookstore. Here we can find a varied array of X-rated home movies, magazines, and even life-size models to use as sexual stimulation. From movies to books to television to real life ("swinging," adultery, teen-age sex and co-ed dorms), sex has taken over as the average American's favorite choice of recreation.

Without a doubt, the American animal is of a unique species. The degree of decadence he takes for granted would be a shock to other, less extraordinary creatures. It is hard to believe that our nation is a mere 200 years old, so ingrained—and so uniform—are our peculiarities.

2

From Topic
to
Controlling Idea

Writing is an orderly yet flexible process that can be divided into three basic stages: prewriting, arrangement, and writing-revising. The prewriting stage is especially important because it is here that you design the framework of your essay. Knowing certain prewriting techniques can help you to move smoothly from a general topic to a limited topic to an angled topic to the major points you will discuss and, finally, to your controlling idea, the keystone of your essay

If your instructor has assigned a topic, this is the logical place for you to begin. Many topics you get in college are fairly specific, requiring you to do something or to answer a question, just as on a short-answer test. Typical of such topics are the following:

1. Essay topic: Is the Death Penalty Cruel and Unusual Punishment?
2. Test question: Discuss three economic causes of the Civil War.
3. Essay topic: What Are the Advantages or Disadvantages of Co-ed Dorms?

Notice that these three topics give you specific directions on what to write. Because the instructors want you to be sure to cover certain areas, they have *limited* and *angled* the topics for you. Learning to recognize topics such as these, which are specific enough to help you plan your essay, will save you time.

Sometimes, however, you will be faced with topics that can't be dealt with in the allotted time and space.

because they are too broad. It is not at all uncommon for a political science teacher to ask a class to write short papers on "The United Nations" or for an engineering instructor to assign a term paper on "The Effects of Engineering on Modern American Culture." Before you can begin discussing topics such as these, you have to narrow them down. If you simply begin writing, hoping for the best, you will probably end up with a disorganized essay made up of one generalization after another. So one of your first jobs is to limit this *general topic* and decide which aspect of it you will focus on.

Limiting and Angling Your Topic

When limiting the topic for a short essay, you might move from the general "A College Course" to the limited "Chemistry" or "History" or "Calculus," or, for a term paper, from "The Rise of Hitler" to "Hitler's Relationship with the Financial Community in Prewar Germany." What you achieve by limiting is a manageable topic, one that you can easily handle in the designated time and space.

In addition to limiting a topic to make it narrower, you will also want to decide from what *angle* you are going to approach your subject. Finding an angle for an essay is like taking a picture. A bland scene can sometimes be made exciting simply by using an unusual camera angle. Deciding on the right approach to a subject can make the difference between a boring essay and an interesting one.

For instance, if you limited your general topic of "A College Course" to "Freshman English," you could slant your essay to talk about the problems you had with your first college English course, or how it was like or unlike your high school English courses. The resulting essay might be informative, but chances are it wouldn't be very absorbing. However, angling that same limited topic to "Freshman English: Blueprint for the Year 2000" or "The Freshman English Course No College Will Offer" or "What Freshman English Can Teach

Ten Year Olds" could yield much more exciting possibilities. What you aim for is the angle that will enable you to write the most complete and interesting essay.

Considering Your Boundaries

Limiting and angling your topic do not take place in a vacuum, however. How narrow your topic should be and from what angle you view it usually depend on the length of your paper, the purpose of your writing, your audience, the occasion, and your knowledge of the subject. The following considerations will help you to determine the boundaries of your assignment and to progress through the prewriting stage of the composing process.

1. **Length**   Most of the time, your instructor will assign a word or page limit for your paper; at other times, the topic itself or the amount of time you have to complete the assignment may suggest its length. Your paper's length will be an important factor in determining your treatment of a topic—you will certainly want to cover a topic in greater depth in a term paper than in a brief essay. A term paper considering floral imagery in Henry James's *The Portrait of a Lady*, for instance, would be longer than an in-class essay on the same topic. In the same way, a topic that you have two weeks to complete should be treated in more depth than one that has to be handed in after two days. If you aren't sure how long to make your paper, discuss your plans with the instructor who assigned it.

2. **Purpose**   The general purpose of a writing task may be to inform, to persuade, or to entertain. An essay or paper can present information, convince a reader of something, entertain the reader with provocative or humorous details, or, frequently, serve some combination of these purposes.

   The purpose of your college writing assignments is usually to show your instructor that you have a good command of the subject. In this case, your purpose is simply to present information. But you may also write to entertain—in letters to friends, for instance—or to persuade—as in an editorial for your college newspaper.

In addition, each of your writing tasks will have a specialized purpose, one unique to the situation at hand. Thus, you may be writing to explain how an experiment was done so that another student may duplicate your procedure, or to evoke sympathy through a description of a childhood tragedy, or to counter your audience's objections to your controversial point of view. Careful consideration of your purpose can help you select and arrange your material.

3. Audience An audience can be one person or a group of individuals, and audiences can vary widely in terms of their education, age, interests, experiences, attitudes, and knowledge of your topic. How well you assess these factors in your intended audience can help to determine the effectiveness of your writing. Of course, audiences can't always be easily characterized; sometimes you will have to search hard for a common denominator in a diverse group. Your college audience is usually an individual—your instructor—although occasionally you may be addressing a group, such as your fellow students. How familiar your audience is with your subject can determine the kind of topic you choose to discuss. A technical discussion of reverse osmosis filters might be fine for a scientific writing class but inappropriate for a freshman composition course. If you aim your essay at a specific audience and keep that audience in mind as you write, your essay will be consistent and focused.

4. Occasion The occasion for your college writing assignments is most often an essay or exam you write in class or a longer paper you write at home. But even for the same topics, different situations require different responses. An in-class essay on inflation for your composition class, for instance, might stress your dif-

ficulty in making ends meet. The same topic discussed
in a short paper for an economics course might emphasize oil revenues and price control. Careful consideration of the occasion for your writing will help give
your essay direction.

5. Knowledge   The amount of knowledge you have
about a subject—and the amount of information you
can reasonably expect to acquire in the time you have
to complete the assignment—will also play a role in
determining your essay's limits and approach. In limiting and angling your topic, therefore, you should consider what aspects of the general subject you are best
qualified to discuss.

One final consideration will also help you to move
from a general topic to one that is limited and angled:
what you want to write about. Your interests and
opinions, the ideas you bring to a subject, are valuable
additions to any essay you write and should influence
the prewriting stage of your essay.

EXERCISE 1

Limit and angle the following topics. In each case,
assume your boundaries are
  1. Length—500 words
  2. Purpose—to present information
  3. Audience—your instructor
  4. Occasion—an essay written at home for your
     writing class
As you limit and angle the topics, try to decide how
each of these boundaries might affect your approach
to the topic. Then, consider your own individual
knowledge of the topic and what aspects of the topic
you would most like to explore.

Example:

General Topic: Sports
Limited Topic: High-School Sports
Angled Topic: Should High-School Girls Com-
                 pete in Contact Sports with Boys?

1. General Topic: TV Shows
   Limited Topic:
   Angled Topic:

2. General Topic: Politics
   Limited Topic:
   Angled Topic:

3. General Topic: Music
   Limited Topic:
   Angled Topic:

4. General Topic: Career Opportunities
   Limited Topic:
   Angled Topic:

Note: In many cases, the angled topic may be suitable for your essay's title.

Deciding What to Write About

Having limited and angled your topic by considering your boundaries, you will want to decide what you have to say about it. There are a number of ways to discover ideas you might have about a subject. We will discuss two of the most common, *listing* and *brainstorming*.

1. Listing Listing works best for topics with which you are very familiar—those you know cold. When you list, you jot down facts and details simply to get them down on paper so that you will be able to choose those that will be most interesting and pertinent. You will not have to search your memory for this information; it should be easily accessible. For instance, if your composition instructor directed the class to write an essay about "What Are the Advantages or Disadvantages of Co-ed Dorms?" and you live in such a dorm, you should be familiar with the living arrangement's advantages and disadvantages. Your first step, then, would be to list as many advantages and disadvantages as you could think of:

Advantages	Disadvantages
1. It's a more true-to-life situation.	1. I would always have to be dressed.
2. The dorms would be more "civilized."	2. There would be too many new social pressures in the dorm.
3. Students would have an opportunity to learn to live around the opposite sex.	3. Each floor would need separate bath facilities.
4. Co-ed dorms would break down stereotyped sex roles.	4. Parents would object.
5. Co-ed dorms would help me feel less homesick.	5. Study habits could be affected.

After making your list, you would choose the category that sounded most interesting and gave you the most to say. If, to you, the advantages of co-ed dorms far outweighed the disadvantages, your decision would be easy. Once you had made this choice, you would then decide how many of these advantages you could discuss in detail. (If your essay was limited to 350 words, you would probably want to write about only two or three of your five advantages. But, if space permitted and you had a lot to say, you could explore all the advantages you listed.) Once you have decided which items on your list would offer you the most to write about, you should have a good idea what your essay is going to be about:

Advantages of Co-ed Dorms
   1. The dorms would probably be more "civilized."
   2. Co-ed dorms would give students an opportunity to learn to live around the opposite sex.
   3. Co-ed dorms would help break down stereotyped sex roles.

Spotting topics like those, for which you can readily think of relevant information, wlil enable you to bypass the brainstorming process and move on to the actual writing of your essay.

2. **Brainstorming**   To brainstorm is to search your mind and jot down in random order all the bits of infor-

mation you can think of about a topic. It is most useful with topics that demand a good deal of thought before you can decide what you want to discuss or when you do not know exactly what you want to write about. It often helps if you can brainstorm your topic with another member of your class or in small groups.

There is no need to record your information in complete sentences; record it as it occurs to you. There is also no need to be selective or judgmental; at this stage, write down everything that comes to mind.

Brainstorming helps you to determine how much you know about a topic. Many times you will recall facts and ideas that you did not even know you had in mind. Brainstorming can also provide a fresh approach to a subject or even suggest new ideas.

If your English instructor asked you to write an essay comparing and contrasting two stories by Edgar Allan Poe that your class had studied during the semester, your brainstorming list—based on your reading of the stories, your class notes, and your own ideas—might look like this:

Essay topic: Compare and contrast Poe's "The Cask of Amontillado" and "The Tell-tale Heart."

- —Both flashbacks—"Cask" fifty years in past ("Heart" more recent?).
- —Both in first person.
- —Narrator of "Heart" confesses and is found out; Montresor, in "Cask," gets away with crime.
- —Both commit murder.
- —Motives: Fortunato insulted Montresor. Old man's eye drove narrator crazy.
- —Did Montresor really have a reason for killing Fortunato, or did he just imagine Fortunato insulted him?
- —Both brutal crimes—Montresor bricks up Fortunato in catacombs; "Heart" narrator dismembers corpse and buries it under floor.
- —Is Montresor sane? Narrator of "Heart" thinks his clever plotting makes him sane.

—Both murders intricately plotted, carefully re-
counted.
—Who is old man in "Heart"? What is significance
of his relationship to narrator?
—"Cask" has dialogue between murderer and vic-
tim; in "Heart" reader never gets to know victim.
—Narrator in "Heart" has acute sense of hearing, is
unusually patient, feels guilty.
—Montresor seems cunning and guilt-free.
—Montresor pretends to be solicitous of victim;
appeals to his vanity.
—Narrator of "Heart" claims to love victim.

Notice that this list is made up of fragments and complete sentences, statements and questions about both
stories. Your task now is to make some sense out of
these bits of information and use them to help you focus
on the points you will stress in your essay. As you consider the items on your list, certain patterns should
begin to emerge. You may find, for instance, that you
have more promising material on the similarities between the two stories than on the differences, and this
would lead you to further angle your topic—with your
instructor's permission—to a comparison between the
two stories. You may even find yourself adding new
details as they occur to you. When your list seems
complete, sort and group the items on it to help you
develop the points that seem most interesting and give
you the most to say. If your essay is limited to between
350 and 500 words, two or three points should be
enough. When you have decided which points will
offer you the most to write about, you have the beginnings of your essay.

"The Cask of Amontillado" and "The Tell-tale Heart":
Murder Most Foul
   1. Each story focuses on a vicious murder moti-
      vated by a desire for revenge.
   2. The two narrators share personality traits that
      lead them to plot their crimes methodically and
      thoroughly.

3. While the narrator in "The Tell-tale Heart" is caught because of his guilt, Montresor in "The Cask of Amontillado" gets away with murder.

EXERCISE 2   Using listing or brainstorming, decide what an essay on each of the following angled topics might be about. In each case, discover as many details as you can that pertain to the topic, and then review your items to decide which three points would be the best to write about in an essay.

1. Angled Topic   Should There Be a Limit on Movie Violence?
   Best Three   1. _____
   Points   2. _____
                     3. _____

2. Angled Topic   Children's TV Programming: An Oasis or a Great
                      Wasteland?
   Best Three   1. _____
   Points   2. _____
                     3. _____

3. Angled Topic   Should Women Be Drafted?
   Best Three   1. _____
   Points   2. _____
                     3. _____

4. Angled Topic   Should Immigration to the United States Be Limited?
   Best Three   1. _____
   Points   2. _____
                     3. _____

5. Angled Topic   What Can Everyone Do to Conserve Energy?
   Best Three   1. _____
   Points   2. _____
                     3. _____

The Controlling Idea

The controlling idea is the main point of your essay. The rest of your essay is devoted to supporting and developing it. Not only does it tell your readers what your essay is about, it tells you, the writer, what you should write about. If your controlling idea is specific enough, you should be able to look at it and find the ideas you will develop in your essay.

There are many different ways you can construct a controlling idea. The first thing you should consider is whether your controlling idea should be *narrow* or *broad*. With a narrow controlling idea you list the specific points to be discussed in your essay; with a broad controlling idea you simply suggest them. If your controlling idea is specific enough, it can serve as a guide as you write your essay.

1. The Narrow Controlling Idea   Formulating the narrow controlling idea requires only that you express the three points you want to discuss in sentence form and in the order in which they will appear in the essay. These points should be listed in order of increasing importance, with the most convincing and important point of your essay presented last. (If you introduce your best point first, the rest of your essay will be a letdown.) Constructing a narrow controlling idea can often be as simple as saying:

> Running is a worthwhile sport not only because it improves muscle tone and lowers the risk of high blood pressure and heart disease, but also because it provides a deep sense of accomplishment.

Beginning writers often feel more comfortable with a narrow controlling idea because they feel that such a definite statement of purpose helps them to keep from wandering from their topics. You may prefer to stay with narrow controlling ideas for a while because they are so simple to construct once you have decided on your essay's main points.

You can express your narrow controlling idea either

in a single sentence or in several sentences. A narrow controlling idea based on the problems of freshman English could be a single sentence that touched on each of your essay's three main points.

> Freshman English is a constant tug-of-war between the needs of average and advanced students, between writing and literature, and between the instructors' enthusiasm for their subjects and most students' lack of that enthusiasm.

Or your narrow controlling idea might mention each point in a separate sentence.

> Freshman English, despite innovative teachers and a flexible curriculum, continues to be beset with problems. Inadequate testing often places superior students in the same class with those needing extensive basic instruction. As a result, instructors are unsure whether to emphasize writing skills or literary appreciation. And on top of all this, they must struggle to overcome students' traditional resentment of the course.

2. The Broad Controlling Idea   When you have mastered the construction of narrow controlling ideas and feel sure you can present your essay's main points clearly and distinctly, you may decide that in some cases it would be better to use a broader, less explicit controlling idea. In an essay exam, a business letter requesting action, or a relatively long research paper, a *narrow controlling idea* often works better, either because it makes the paper easier to follow, or because it is more direct. In other cases, particularly in short essays where you and your readers can keep track of the argument more easily, a *broad controlling idea* may be more effective.

While a *narrow controlling idea* states the points of your essay, a *broad controlling idea* implies them—that is, suggests them without stating them in so many words. Even so, your readers should be able to form a fairly specific and accurate idea of what the rest of the essay is going to be about, and see clearly that the points you discuss are relevant to your controlling idea. A statement like the following one, for example, could sum up the three problems of freshman English.

Freshman English is perhaps the most controversial course in the college curriculum.

While not specifying the exact points the essay will discuss, this broad controlling idea is still specific enough to be supported by the three problems we have listed. The chart below gives further examples of *narrow* and *broad* controlling ideas.

Narrow Controlling Idea	Broad Controlling Idea
1. The major difficulties of keeping a salt water aquarium are the expense of the equipment, the problem of maintaining proper salt levels, and the delicacy of the fish.	While raising salt water fish is an exciting experience, anyone considering this hobby should consider its drawbacks.
2. Curing the common everyday headache is not as simple as it sounds because headaches fall into several distinct categories, each having its own peculiarities. Migraines, tension headaches, and cluster headaches are three of the most troublesome kinds.	Headaches are difficult to treat because each kind of headache has its own patterns. Only by knowing these patterns can a physician prescribe an appropriate cure.
3. Within the past fifteen years two movies, Andy Warhol's *Frankenstein* and Mel Brooks' *Young Frankenstein*, have illustrated the changing dimensions of Mary Shelley's original myth.	The movies have taken Mary Shelley's nineteenth-century allegory about man and technology and adapted it to mirror the current American attitude toward science.

EXERCISE 3   In each of the following instances, go through as many steps as you need to create narrow and broad controlling ideas for the topics provided. In some cases, you will need to consider your essay's boundaries (follow the guidelines in Exercise 1) before listing or brainstorming. In others, listing or brainstorming alone will be sufficient.

1. Angled Topic   Why Are There So Many Soap Operas on TV?
    Best Three   1. They attract a large viewing audience.
    Points   2. They sell sponsors' products.
                3. They are the only source of daytime drama.

    Narrow _____
    Controlling _____
    Idea _____
    Broad _____
    Controlling _____
    Idea _____

2. Angled Topic   Is the Death Penalty Cruel and Unusual Punishment?
    Best Three   1. _____
    Points   2. _____
               3. _____

    Narrow _____
    Controlling _____
    Idea _____
    Broad _____
    Controlling _____
    Idea _____

3. General Topic   Controversial Legislation
    Limited Topic   Gun Control
    Angled Topic   The Possible Results of Gun Control
    Best Three   1. Fewer accidental shootings.
    Points   2. Increased police power.
               3. Fewer gun-related crimes.

    Narrow _____
    Controlling _____
    Idea _____
    Broad _____
    Controlling _____
    Idea _____

4. General Topic   Hobbies
   Limited Topic   _____
   Angled Topic   _____
   Best Three   1. _____
   Points   2. _____
                 3. _____

   Narrow   _____
   Controlling   _____
   Idea
   Broad   _____
   Controlling   _____
   Idea

Keep these points in mind about the controlling idea:
1. <u>Your controlling idea should cover, either by implication or specifically, all the main points to be discussed in your essay.</u> A controlling idea that ignores an important point can de-emphasize that point, and, as a result, confuse your readers.

    For instance, let us suppose you want to convince your readers that bicycles are better than cars for getting around in the city, and that your three main points are:
    1. Bicycles do not pollute.
    2. Bicycles are more maneuverable in traffic.
    3. Bicycles are easy to park.
A *broad* controlling idea that says "Bicycles are superior to cars for city driving because they are smaller" would include only points 2 and 3; point 1 would then seem irrelevant in your essay. Of course, because bicycles are small they are easier to park and maneuver, but this has nothing to do with the fact that they do not pollute the air. It is easier to see that a *narrow* controlling idea that mentions only two of your three main points would also confuse your readers. For your controlling idea to do its job in the essay, it must include, either implicitly or explicitly, *all* the main points your readers will find in the body of your essay.

2. <u>Your controlling idea should refer *only* to the points the essay will cover.</u> Announcing to your readers that bicycles are superior because they are cheaper, cleaner, quieter, and better for the environment, and then discussing only the last of these points—or introducing additional ones—will undermine your arguments, because readers will blame you for promising in the controlling idea more than your essay delivers.

3. <u>Your controlling idea, even if it is merely implied, should be specific enough to give your essay its direction.</u> A sentence like "Bicycles are better than cars for many reasons, as I will show in this essay" does *not* give a clear sense of where your essay will go.

EXERCISE 4

Before you go on to Chapter 3, make sure you can define the following terms in your own words:
1. General topic
2. Limited topic
3. Angled topic
4. Boundaries
5. Brainstorming list
6. Narrow controlling idea
7. Broad controlling idea

CHAPTER 3

Structuring Your Essay

The easiest way to structure your writing is to plan the essay directly around your controlling idea. If you use it as a starting point, you will find a straightforward and unified essay easier to plan and execute.

The Narrow Controlling Idea

Suppose that your composition instructor has assigned an essay about the worst job you ever had. Because this topic requires you to search your memory, you decide to brainstorm. You compile a brainstorming list that includes all the details you can recall; you sort and group the bits of information, eliminate irrelevant items, and settle on the three points on which you want your essay to focus. After a bit of thought, you arrive at this narrow controlling idea:

> Working on the assembly line was no picnic because the work was monotonous, my foreman hated me, and I had to work the midnight-to-eight shift.

From this *narrow controlling idea* you now can outline the rest of your essay. Each of the three parts of your controlling idea is a point you are going to discuss in your essay. And each point can be made into a topic sentence that will define what one of the body paragraphs of your essay will be about. In addition, you will use the relevant items on your brainstorming list (as well as any new details that occur to you) when you are developing your body paragraphs.

If your introductory paragraph ended with the

narrow controlling idea above, your three body paragraphs could be set up like this:

1. <u>Topic sentence:</u> "The monotony of the assembly line really got to me after a while." <u>Supporting detail:</u> In this paragraph you would describe the minute, boring task you performed, emphasizing the sameness, the way the assembly line never seemed to let up, how slowly time passed, and how few breaks you could take.

2. <u>Topic sentence:</u> "Things might have been better if only my foreman hadn't been so hostile to me." <u>Supporting detail:</u> Here you would discuss the specific ways in which your foreman discriminated against you, spoke harshly to you, or otherwise made your working life miserable.

3. <u>Topic sentence:</u> "The very worst part of this horrible job was the hours." <u>Supporting detail:</u> Now you mention how lonely it was on the job at night, how dangerous it was on the streets at night, and how working this shift threw your whole life off balance.

Remember, the diagram of a short essay should look something like this:

Title

General introductory remarks ⎯⎯⎯⎯⎯

⎯⎯⎯⎯⎯→ narrow controlling idea.

Topic sentence (first main point) ⎯⎯⎯

⎯⎯⎯⎯⎯→ supporting detail.

Topic sentence (second main point) ⎯⎯⎯

⎯⎯⎯⎯⎯→ supporting detail.

> Topic sentence (third main point) _____
> _____
> _____ → supporting detail.

> Restatement of controlling idea _____
> _____ → general
> concluding remarks _____
> _____ → final statement.

A more detailed diagram of your essay-in-progress would look like this:

The Worst Job I Ever Had

Narrow
Controlling
Idea

> Introductory remarks _____
> _____ → Working on the assembly line was no picnic because (1) the work was monotonous, (2) my foreman hated me, and (3) I had to work the midnight-to-eight shift.

Topic
Sentence

> The monotony of the assembly line really got to me after a while. (Paraphrase of "1") _____
> _____ → Supporting detail.

Topic
Sentence

> Things might have been better if only my foreman hadn't been so hostile to me. (Paraphrase of "2") _____ → Supporting detail.

Topic
Sentence

> The very worst part of this horrible job was the hours. (Paraphrase of "3") _____
> _____ → Supporting detail.

Restatement
Between the inconvenient hours, the constant conflicts with the foreman, and the tedious work, my job was a nightmare. ──────────

────────────► Concluding remarks.

Here is a possible final version of this essay, which you can see also conforms to the pattern. Notice how the topic sentences of the three body paragraphs support and develop the different parts of the narrow controlling idea.

Title

The Worst Job I Ever Had

Introductory Remarks

Narrow Controlling Idea

Last summer I had the misfortune to work on the assembly line at an automotive plant. While the pay was excellent, the working conditions were so bad I couldn't wait for the summer to end. Working on the assembly line was no picnic because the work was monotonous, my foreman hated me, and I had to work the midnight-to-eight shift.

Topic Sentence

Support

The monotony of the assembly line really got to me after a while. Day after day, hour after hour, I performed the same task again and again. All I had to do was tighten one bolt: pick up my wrench, turn my wrist, and move on to the next bolt. I got to the point where I was counting the minutes till it was time to punch out. And hardly ever could I take a break to unwind or rest.

Topic Sentence

Things might have been better if my foreman hadn't been so hostile to me. As soon as he found out I was a "college kid," he proceeded to make

Support

my life difficult. Not only did he deny me the breaks I deserved, but he never missed an opportunity to make a sarcastic crack about the length of my hair, the way I dressed, or the fact that I was majoring in art history. Before long I began to dread coming to work.

Topic
Sentence

The very worst part of this horrible job was the hours. Since I was hired as temporary help, I had last choice when it came to shifts. Naturally, I got stuck with midnight-to-eight. The plant was really lonely at night, even when the other workers were around. Getting to my job was really dangerous. I was nearly always alone on the bus, and had to walk several long, dark blocks alone from the bus stop. Besides, my crazy schedule made any social life just about impossible.

Support

Restatement

Between the inconvenient hours, the constant conflicts with the foreman, and the tedious work, my job was a nightmare. True, the pay was great, and I learned a lot about tightening bolts, but I know I'll do everything possible to avoid working the night shift in a factory again.

Concluding
Remarks

The Broad Controlling Idea

Structuring your essay by using a *broad controlling idea* is no different from structuring it with a narrow controlling idea. Even though the broad controlling idea does not mention the specific points to be discussed, it should usually imply them. By glancing back at your list of the three main points you will be writing about, you can readily structure your essay. While these points are not specifically stated in your controlling idea, they will be mentioned one by one in your essay.

Suppose your instructor in modern European history gave you the following assignment for a midterm:

> During the 1850s and 1860s, both Germany and Italy went through processes of national unification. Choose *one* of these two countries, and outline the process by which it moved from a group of separate states or provinces into a unified nation.

Some initial thinking tells you that you can write a stronger essay on Italy than on Germany; thus, limiting your topic is almost automatic. Since the topic is already angled for you, you are ready to brainstorm. In making your list, you try to recall details from your class and your textbook. After a while, you settle on the three main divisions of your essay on the unification of Italy:

1. Role played by Mazzini
2. Role played by Cavour
3. Role played by Garibaldi

A broad controlling idea describing what it is you intend to write about could be:

> Three men in particular worked to make the dream of a unified Italy a reality.

The detailed schematic diagram would look something like this:

Title	The Unification of Italy
Broad Controlling Idea	Introductory remarks ——————— ——————→ Three men in particular worked to make the dream of a unified Italy a reality.
Topic Sentence	The groundwork was laid by Giuseppe Mazzini, founder of a society called Young Italy——— ———————————→ supporting detail

Topic
Sentence

> ⌐ The efforts toward unification were continued
> by Camillo Benso di Cavour, prime minister of
> Sardinia during the 1850s _____
> _____ ⟶ supporting detail.

Topic
Sentence

> ⌐ The unification of Italy was completed by Giu-
> seppe Garibaldi, a popular revolutionary national-
> ist. _____
> _____ ⟶ supporting detail.

Restatement

> ⌐ As a result of the efforts of three men, the col-
> lection of provinces that the Austrian statesman
> Metternich had referred to as a "geographical ex-
> pression" eventually became a unified country.
> _____
> _____ ⟶ concluding remarks

Notice how the major points of your essay can all be
derived from the broad controlling idea. The essay
structured around this *broad controlling idea* would
look like this.

Title   The Unification of Italy

Introductory
Remarks

> ⌐ One of the major events of the nineteenth cen-
> tury was the unification of Italy, which before the
> mid-1800s was divided into different city-states.
> As of 1815, control of two provinces, Lombardy
> and Venezia, was in the hands of Austria, others
> were ruled by French or Italian kings, and still
> others, in the area around Rome, were governed by
> the papacy. By midcentury, however, more and

Controlling
Idea

> more Italians became committed to the idea of uni-
> fication. Three men in particular worked to make
> the dream of a unified Italy a reality.

Topic
Sentence

The groundwork was laid by Giuseppe Mazzini, founder of a society called Young Italy. This group was devoted to encouraging a revolution throughout Italy—a revolution whose cause was nationalism. Mazzini's democratic republic was to be founded on principles of universal suffrage and was, therefore, to reflect the true desires of the

Support

people. Italy's liberals, however, hoped that the unification of Italy could be achieved through a constitutional monarchy, which could unite the many existing monarchical and papal states. Because they did not support Mazzini's "radical" idea of a republic, his cause failed.

Topic
Sentence

The efforts toward unification were continued by Camillo Benso di Cavour, prime minister of Sardinia during the 1850s. Cavour, a monarchist, was not sympathetic to Mazzini's revolutionary and republican ideas. His goal was not to unify all of Italy, but only the northern Italian states. Powerful Austria still controlled the northern provinces

Support

of Lombardy and Venezia, and so Cavour enlisted the aid of Napoleon III and the French army against Austria. As a result, Sardinia was able to acquire Lombardy. Meanwhile, central Italy's nationalists were demonstrating for a unified Italy. Leaders advocated union with Sardinia, and thus Cavour's goal of a unified northern Italy was achieved.

Topic
Sentence

The unification of Italy was completed by Giuseppe Garibaldi, a popular revolutionary nationalist. Leading a guerrilla band of "Red Shirts," Garibaldi landed in Sicily in 1860 and took the city of Palermo. But before he could reach Rome, Cavour, who feared confrontation there with the

Support

pope and the French army, sent Sardinian troops to check Garibaldi's advance. When the people in Sicily and the papal states voted to join with Sardinia, Garibaldi accepted their decision. The new kingdom of Italy, a parliamentary monarchy under King Victor Emmanuel II, was born.

Restatement

Concluding
remarks

As a result of the efforts of three men, the collection of provinces that the Austrian statesman Metternich had referred to as a "geographical expression" eventually became a unified country. Social and economic divisions remained, but the country was one nation.

Whether you use a broad controlling idea or a narrow one is up to you. In the case of the short essay above, listing the men's names and titles in the first paragraph would have been tedious and unnecessary. It was enough to use a broad controlling idea that referred to "three men" and did not belabor the issue by identifying them one by one.

As you can see, then, the situation determines what type of controlling idea you will use. Some types of writing, like informal essays and personal letters, call for subtlety. Others, like term papers and reports, demand just the opposite: a structure that is clear and obvious. Whether you use a broad controlling idea or a narrow one, the organizing process is the same. If your controlling idea is specific enough, structuring and writing a well-unified essay should be much easier than you expect it to be.

EXERCISE 1

The following diagram outlines an essay on the topic "Contemporary Films: Escape for the Masses." Here you have the narrow controlling idea, three topic sentences derived from it, and the beginning of the concluding paragraph. Now try to fill in the introductory remarks, the supporting detail in the body paragraphs, and the concluding remarks.

Contemporary Films: Escape for the Masses

Introductory
Remarks

Narrow
Controlling
Idea

Westerns, romantic dramas, and science fiction, three movie genres, owe their popularity to the public's need to escape reality.

Topic
Sentence

Westerns, often set in the idyllic past, make an appealing statement about the integrity of the individual.

Support

Topic
Sentence

Romantic films, with their glamorous settings and invariably **happy endings, appeal** to many.

Support

Topic
Sentence

Science-fiction movies, set in the future, provide the ultimate escape for viewers.

Support

Restatement

| Each of these film genres fills a need for Americans—a need for escape from the pressures of their complicated lives.

Concluding
Remarks

Notice that the conclusion, as is often the case, restates only the broad controlling idea. Readers will immediately see that the phrase "each of these three film genres" sums up the essay's main divisions.

EXERCISE 2

The next diagram is a plan for an essay on the topic "Should the United States Continue Space Exploration?" Here only the narrow controlling idea and the restatement of this idea in the concluding paragraph are supplied for you. Fill in the topic sentences for the body paragraphs, and then complete the essay.

Title   Why the U.S. Space Program Is a Necessity

Introductory
Remarks
Narrow
Controlling
Idea

Even though it is expensive, the U.S. space program is well worth the money. First, it has provided a great amount of spin-off technology useful in areas such as medicine. Second, the space program has greatly enlarged our knowledge of earth. Finally, exploration of space has given us a new frontier to strive for.

Topic
Sentence

Support

Topic
Sentence

Support

Topic
Sentence

Support

Restatement

Concluding
Remarks

> ⌐ Because of its many benefits, the space program
> should continue to be funded in this country.

EXERCISE 3   Consider the difficulties encountered by people who
are short, tall, nearsighted, left-handed, or overweight.
Choose one of these conditions and, working with the
limited and angled topic "Problems Faced by _____
People," brainstorm or list to decide on the three most
compelling problems. Then, construct an appropriate
broad controlling idea. Finally, write your three examples of problems in the numbered spaces.

Broad controlling idea: _____

Three supporting examples:

1. _____
2. _____
3. _____

On the following essay diagram, fill in your broad
controlling idea and topic sentences for the three body
paragraphs. When you have finished, fill in the rest of
the essay.

Title   _____

Introductory
Remarks

Broad
Controlling
Idea

Topic
Sentence

Support

Topic
Sentence

Support

Topic
Sentence

Support

Restatement

Concluding
Remarks

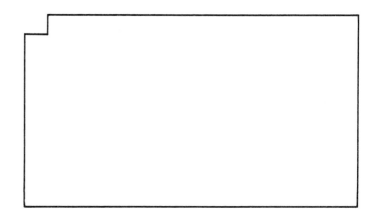

REVIEW

The steps that you have just been practicing are those you follow before you begin to write any essay. This prewriting phase of your work is extremely important, because it is here that you organize the material you are going to write about and draw it together in a coherent structure. Each time you prepare to write an essay, then, remember to consider your assignment's boundaries, limit and angle your topic, list or brainstorm to decide on your essay's major points, and develop a narrow or broad controlling idea. Next, use the individual points of your controlling idea for your topic sentences. After this step, consult the information you obtained by listing or brainstorming for supporting detail to develop your body paragraphs. Finally, if you have not already done so, give your essay a descriptive title.

This same technique can be used very effectively in constructing an answer for an essay exam. Here is a detailed diagram of an answer to the question "Discuss how three science fiction writers we have read this term make special use of point of view in their novels":

Introductory
Remarks

George Bernard Shaw once said that when he got to Scotland, he was taken by the charming qualities of the ordinary; everything was new and different. To his surprise, when he returned to his own country, he found that it too had all these things. Shaw was not thinking about science fiction, but his reasoning still applies. To really examine human mores and emotions, you would have to be outside them. By using a unique point of view, that of an alien, science fiction writers can travel outside their own houses so as to see them better when they return. <u>Three books, Arthur Clarke's</u> *Childhood's End*, <u>Robert Heinlein's *Stranger in a Strange Land*, and Ursula K. LeGuin's *Left Hand of Darkness*, illustrate this use of point of view.</u>

Narrow Controlling Idea *(margin label)*

Topic Sentence *(margin label)*

<u>Because of his unique position as an alien, Karellan, in Arthur Clarke's *Childhood's End*, is able to analyze earth culture objectively.</u>

[Appropriate supporting detail, based on your own reading and interpretation, would follow.]

Topic Sentence *(margin label)*

<u>Mike, the main character of Heinlein's *Stranger in a Strange Land*, makes an even more detailed examination of mankind.</u>

[Supporting detail.]

Topic Sentence *(margin label)*

<u>Perhaps the most subtle and far-reaching comment on man is provided by the interplay of a hermaphroditic alien and a human in Ursula K. LeGuin's *Left Hand of Darkness*.</u>

[Supporting detail.]

Restatement

Concluding
Remarks

> It is my belief that science fiction's greatest strength lies in its ability to use an outsider's point of view to examine humanity. Without this, science fiction becomes just another form of storytelling, a space opera set against an exotic backdrop. As the three books I have discussed illustrate, it can be, and often is, much more than that.

Now the student taking the exam has to fill in the body paragraphs with relevant supporting details. Once this is done, he or she will have a very tight answer that presents its information in a direct and easily understandable form.

Common Structuring Patterns

As we have indicated, the form your essay takes depends on your controlling idea and your assignment. Usually you do not decide upon a pattern of development in advance; it derives naturally from your material. Other times your assignment tells you how to shape your essay.

Compare and contrast the strengths and weaknesses of objective and subjective testing.

Discuss three reasons for the increasing salt content of the lower Delaware River.

The patterns of organization we are going to present are the ones that you will encounter most often in your college writing. By familiarizing yourself with these patterns, you will learn to recognize them and to use them when they are indicated by your material and your controlling idea.

1. **Illustration**   Many controlling ideas are statements that are best clarified and supported by examples. Because the most common way of explaining an idea

to someone is to give examples, illustration is used in almost every academic situation. Examples can persuade your readers, and they can also add life to an otherwise dull presentation.

In an essay structured around illustration, your introduction presents your controlling idea and your body paragraphs present specific examples to support it. Your conclusion restates your controlling idea and reinforces the major point your examples have supported.

¶1 Introduction
¶2 First example
¶3 Second example
¶4 Third example
¶5 Conclusion

The following controlling idea calls for an illustration pattern:

During the past five years, three programs have shown how innovative and informative public television can be.

An outline of an illustration essay based on this controlling idea would look like this:

¶1 Introduction—During the past five years, three programs have shown how innovative and informative public television can be.
¶2 First example—"Washington Week in Review"
¶3 Second example—"Masterpiece Theatre"
¶4 Third example—"Sesame Street"
¶5 Conclusion

2. Comparison-Contrast   A *comparison* shows how two or more things are alike, and a *contrast* shows how they are different. Because comparing and contrasting things are basic to our thinking, this pattern is used extensively in midterms, final exams, and papers. When you read questions, certain words and phrases signal

that the comparison-contrast pattern is called for—"compare and contrast," "differentiate between advantages and disadvantages," and so forth. When preparing to write a comparison-contrast paper you should make sure that you discuss properties shared by both subjects.

There are two possible arrangements of comparison contrast essays, a *subject-by-subject comparison* and a *point-by-point comparison.* In a subject-by-subject comparison you discuss all of subject A and then all of subject B. Subject-by-subject comparisons are good for short papers, where a reader can remember all the points you are making about each subject. The following outline illustrates a subject-by-subject comparison:

¶1 Introduction—Controlling idea
¶2 Subject A
    Point 1
    Point 2
¶3 Subject B
    Point 1
    Point 2
¶4 Conclusion

In a point-by-point comparison, you organize your paper around points, not subjects. Each section of your paper discusses a single point shared by both subject A and subject B. First you make a point about one subject and then follow it with a point about the other. This pattern of organization is preferable for long papers because it enables readers to see each point of comparison separately and to keep track of these points. A point-by-point comparison would look like this:

¶1 Introduction
¶2 Point 1 Subject A
    Point 1 Subject B
¶3 Point 2 Subject A
    Point 2 Subject B
¶4 Point 3 Subject A
    Point 3 Subject B
¶5 Conclusion

The following controlling idea calls for a comparison-contrast pattern.

> Marlow and Kurtz in Conrad's *Heart of Darkness* are both innocent when they enter the jungle, but they react to their experiences in different ways.

Notice that this controlling idea stresses the differences between Marlow and Kurtz. In all comparison-contrast essays, your controlling idea must indicate whether you are stressing similarities or differences.

An outline of a subject-by-subject comparison essay organized around this controlling idea would look like this:

¶1 Introduction—Marlow and Kurtz are both innocent when they enter the jungle, but they react to their experiences in different ways.

¶2 Marlow
  Resists the wilderness
  Learns from his experience
  Survives his ordeal

¶3 Kurtz
  Gives in to the wilderness
  Learns little about himself from the experience
  Dies as a result of his ordeal

¶4 Conclusion

3. Cause and Effect   Many academic assignments require you to trace causes or to predict effects. Often, your topic as well as your controlling idea will contain certain key words that will tell you to structure your essay this way: "discuss causes," "discuss factors," "outline the effects," "assess the implications."

Essays of this pattern may be organized around either causes or effects or around both. The introduction contains a controlling idea that identifies a cause and its effects or an effect and its causes. The body paragraphs list causes or effects, and the conclusion summarizes your major points.

¶1 Introduction
¶2 First cause or effect
¶3 Second cause or effect
¶4 Third cause or effect
¶5 Conclusion

The following controlling idea would call for a cause-and-effect structure.

Heterogeneous classroom grouping can have a positive effect on students.

An outline for a cause-and-effect essay based on this controlling idea would look like this:

¶1 Introduction—Heterogeneous classroom grouping can have a positive effect on students
¶2 First effect—Increases flexibility of students
¶3 Second effect—Increases social skills of students
¶4 Third effect—Increases the learning ability of students
¶5 Conclusion

4. Classification and Division Whether taking bits of information and *classifying* them into one group or another or taking a mass of information and *dividing* it into categories, you will often use classification and division patterns in your college writing. Science courses, marketing courses, and literature courses frequently ask you to divide or classify information.

Classification or division essays are organized around a controlling idea that indicates into which categories or classes your subject is divided or classified. The body of your essay presents each of the categories or classes in turn, and your conclusion reinforces the controlling idea. An outline for a short classification or division paper would look like this:

¶1 Introduction—Controlling idea indicating classification or division.

¶2 First category or class
¶3 Second category or class
¶4 Third category or class
¶5 Conclusion

The following controlling idea calls for a classification-division pattern:

Heroes in our society can be classified into three categories.

An essay based on this controlling idea would use the pattern we discussed.

¶1 Introduction—Heroes in our society can be classified into three categories
¶2 First kind of hero
¶3 Second kind of hero
¶4 Third kind of hero
¶5 Conclusion

5. **Process** The purpose of a process essay is to help a reader understand the steps or stages of a procedure. In a political-science class you might use a process pattern to explain how a case reaches the Supreme Court; in a chemistry lab you might use this pattern to explain how you carry out a certain experiment.

Like all the essay patterns we have discussed, process essays consist of an introduction, body, and conclusion. The introduction usually provides an overview of the process and presents your controlling idea. Each body paragraph treats one major stage of the procedure. Steps are described in logical sequence and, in most cases, in strict chronological order. Your conclusion reviews the basic steps in the procedure and reinforces any points you want to make.

¶1 Introduction—Controlling idea
¶2 Step 1
¶3 Step 2
¶4 Step 3
¶5 Conclusion—Reinforcing major points

The following thesis would call for a process pattern of organization:

Quantitative data analysis consists of four basic steps: gathering data, devising a program of analysis, running the program, and studying the results.

An outline of a short paper based on this controlling idea would look like this:

¶1 Introduction—Quantitative data analysis consists of four basic steps: gathering data, devising a program of analysis, running the program, and studying the results
¶2 Step 1—Gathering data
¶3 Step 2—Devising a program of analysis
¶4 Step 3—Running the program
¶5 Step 4—Studying the results
¶6 Conclusion—Reinforcing major points

REVIEW EXERCISE   For each of the following series of broad or narrow controlling ideas, brainstorm or list to decide on three specific points that will provide the necessary support for an essay.

1. Soap operas can provide a valuable educational experience for the open-minded viewer. Not only do they offer a fairly realistic view of middle-class concerns and desires, but they also provide a viewer with fairly good drama.

   [In what ways can they do this?]
   Reason 1. _____
   Reason 2. _____
   Reason 3. _____

2. The creature that emerged from the swamp was easily the most grotesque and horrifying being any of us had ever seen.

[What things were so horrible about the swamp creature?]
Aspect 1. ———————————————————
Aspect 2. ———————————————————
Aspect 3. ———————————————————

3. Even though Clive and I are now ecstatically happy together, the tortured face of Bruce still haunts me, reminding me of the life I faced as wife of a Warlock.

[What are the difficulties of being married to a member of a motorcycle gang?]
Problem 1. ———————————————————
Problem 2. ———————————————————
Problem 3. ———————————————————

4. Since Dry Gulch was invaded by locusts in 1902, the population of the town has changed considerably.

[How have the locusts changed Dry Gulch?]
Result 1. ———————————————————
Result 2. ———————————————————
Result 3. ———————————————————

5. There are several causes of student apathy in national elections.

[What are the causes of student apathy?]
Cause 1. ———————————————————
Cause 2. ———————————————————
Cause 3. ———————————————————

6. Citizens of the quaint town of Katonah are advancing suggestions on how it can overcome its image as a sleepy little fishing village.

[How are the townspeople attempting to solve this problem?]
Solution 1. ———————————————————
Solution 2. ———————————————————
Solution 3. ———————————————————

7. All comic books are not alike; in fact, neither are the people who read them. Superhero comics, romance comics, and horror comics attract radically different readers.

[How are they different?]
Kind 1. _____
Kind 2. _____
Kind 3. _____

Choose any one of the controlling ideas above and use your three points about it to construct three possible topic sentences for an essay's body paragraphs. Then complete the essay.

4

Revising
Your
Essay

As the word itself indicates, *revision* is the process of looking again at what you have written and changing parts in order to make your essay conform more accurately to your purpose and intended meaning. Revision takes place at *every* stage of the composing process. At the same time you are considering the shape your essay will take you are also arriving at new ideas. Similarly, when you write your essay you are also altering ideas and considering arrangement. Some changes you make may be small, such as adding a word or phrase; some may be major, such as rewriting whole paragraphs or deleting sections of your paper. Whatever the case, remember that the revision process is a series of concerns that occur throughout the writing of your essay.

Usually the first draft of your essay is nothing more than a rough copy that needs work before it is ready for an audience. You have written it intent upon getting down your ideas and not worrying very much about structure or style. Often, your rough draft may have to be revised several times. As strange as it may seem, you should begin to revise by putting your paper aside for an hour, a day, even a week, if your deadline permits it. This "cooling off" period lets you disengage yourself from what you have written and view it more objectively. Then, when you come back to it, you may find it easier to read your essay critically and see what changes you should make. Keeping in mind your audience, purpose, length, occasion, and knowledge of the subject, you fine-tune your presentation.

You should be careful not to confuse editing and revising. When you edit, you are concerned with the mechanics and grammar of your paper. When you revise, you focus upon the *general structure, paragraphs,* and *sentences and words* of your essay. During your revision you make sure that you have organized your essay effectively, and that you have included a controlling idea. Next, you check that each paragraph performs its function and that you have used explicit topic sentences. Finally, you ensure that your sentences and words effectively convey the meaning of your ideas. You reject some words, substitute others, and experiment with sentence structure and word order. Although we discuss each of these concerns separately, it is a mistake to assume that you only have one objective in mind each time you read a draft of your essay. A number of these objectives are present each time you read your essay but in different proportion, depending on your concerns at a given stage of the composing process.

The following checklist might help you begin your revisions of general structure:

Organization

Does your essay have:

A title?
An introduction?
A body?
A conclusion?
A controlling idea?
Topic sentences?
A restatement of the controlling idea in the conclusion?

Here are the rough draft and two revisions, with teacher's comments, of a student's essay. Notice how, with each revision, the essay becomes clearer and more effective and the illustration pattern becomes more explicit:

Comments

Good introduction.

Controlling idea lists points to be discussed.

Only one body paragraph? Also, it has nothing to do with controlling idea.

Conclusion is effective, but doesn't restate the controlling idea—can it be salvaged?

Rough Draft

I chose pharmacy as my major in college because I felt it was an open field. Once you get your degree and become a registered pharmacist, you have many opportunities open to you. You can work in hospitals, in research companies, or in your own pharmacy.

I have talked with many registered pharmacists and they told me how good the field is. Before I decided on this career, I worked two years in a pharmacy. As you can see, I knew something about the profession before I enrolled.

Pharmacy is not a trade or an ordinary job. It is a profession to be proud of. A pharmacist aids people when they are sick and is a valuable member of any health delivery team. I feel that as a pharmacist, I will not only help myself and my family, but my community as well.

You've got plenty of useful information here, and I can get a lot from it. But you have some problems with organization and development. You have a nice controlling idea at the end of your first paragraph—it lists all the points that should be discussed in the rest of your essay. According to you, graduate pharmacists can work in hospitals, work in research, or open their own businesses. But instead of developing these examples in the body of your essay, you go on to discuss something else. In addition, your conclusion is completely unrelated to the controlling idea. You've got a lot of revising to do here— keep the introduction and use its controlling idea to structure your next draft.

Revision 1

Title?

I chose pharmacy as my major in college because I felt it was an open field. Once you get your degree and become a registered pharmacist, you have many opportunities open to you. You can work in hospitals, in research companies, or in your own pharmacy.

Much better. The body paragraphs now support the controlling idea.

Pharmacists are an integral part of the health delivery system. Not only do the hospital pharmacists do a great deal of work, they also have a lot of responsibility. They usually are in charge of all medicine coming in and going out of the hospital pharmacy. In some hospitals, they even run in-service courses about drugs for nurses and doctors.

Topic sentences are weak. You need a firmer, more direct statement of the points to be discussed in each body paragraph.

Both private companies and federal agencies use pharmacists when conducting tests on the many new drugs that are introduced each year. Along with chemists, biologists, and physicians, pharmacists assist in keeping drugs with dangerous side effects off the market.

My uncle owns a pharmacy and makes a good living. Working for him for the past two years, I have been able to see how interesting running your own pharmacy can be. Many times my uncle is the only person his customers see who will explain to them what their prescriptions are for. They trust him and often come to him for advice.

Good restatement of controlling idea. This is a well-structured conclusion.

As you can see, there are many opportunities for a graduate pharmacist. It is for this reason that I view pharmacy as being more than just an ordinary job. It is a profession to be proud of. A pharmacist aids people when they are in need. I feel that, as a pharmacist, I will not only help myself and my family, but my community as well.

This revision has done a lot for the original essay. Now you're discussing each point of your controlling idea in your body paragraphs, and the whole essay is balanced. You've also managed to develop the original three paragraphs into five, and each part of the essay now does what it's supposed to do. The main problem with this draft is that your body paragraphs still need more definite topic sentences. Also, how about a descriptive title, to let your readers know what you're going to discuss, and maybe even arouse their interest? One more draft should do it!

Revision 2

Pharmacy: A Growing Field

I chose pharmacy as my major in college because I felt it was an open field. Once you get your degree and become a registered pharmacist, you have many opportunities open to you. You can work in hospitals, research companies, or your own pharmacy.

Most large hospitals are always in need of pharmacists, because hospital pharmacists are important members of the health delivery system. Not only do they do a great deal of work, they also have a lot of responsibility. They usually are in charge of all medicine coming in and going out of the hospital pharmacy. In some hospitals, they even run in-service courses about drugs for nurses and doctors.

Topic sentences link up nicely with your controlling idea, and with the paragraphs they introduce in this draft.

Both private research companies and federal agencies also need to hire many pharmacists. These companies use pharmacists to conduct tests on the many new drugs that are introduced each year. Along with chemists, biologists, and physicians, pharmacists assist in keeping drugs with dangerous side effects off the market.

There is also a need for small neighborhood pharmacies. My uncle owns one and makes a good living. Working for him for the past two years, I have been able to see how interesting running your own pharmacy can be. Many times my uncle is the only person his customers can come to for information about pharmaceuticals. They trust him and often come to him for advice.

As you can see, there are many opportunities for a graduate pharmacist. It is for this reason that I view pharmacy as being more than just an ordinary job. It is a profession to be proud of. A pharmacist aids people when they are in need. I feel that, as a pharmacist, I will not only help myself and my family, but my community as well.

EXERCISE

Take a paper you have written and see if it needs revision. Use the checklist on page 56 to help you decide.

THE
PARAGRAPHS

Section II discusses the different techniques for writing introductory, body, and concluding paragraphs. Each kind of paragraph has a chapter of its own, but each is related in its purpose to the others. If an introduction, a body paragraph, or a conclusion does not do what it is supposed to do, the rest of the essay, no matter how well written, will suffer. Because all the paragraphs in an essay interact, none should be treated as though it were isolated from the others.

CHAPTER 5

The
Introductory
Paragraph

What It Does

Remember, the general purpose of an opening paragraph is to ease the reader into the essay and, in the process, establish your controlling idea. The paragraph should attract your readers' attention, and make them want to read on. It should also make clear what the rest of the essay is going to be about. One sentence is simply not enough to do all this: the introduction to an essay should be a carefully thought out and well-constructed paragraph.

1. Attracting Attention Try to begin your introduction with a remark that is likely to arouse interest and curiosity in your readers. One tactic is to take the rather ordinary generalization that is likely to come first to mind and try to make it more concrete and vivid. For instance, look at these initial sentences of an introductory paragraph:

> Every time I pick up the paper I read about crime in the streets. Something has to be done.

With some imagination, this bland opening can be turned into a varied and exciting one:

> "Man shot as he waited for a bus." "Shopper mugged as she approached her car." "Children beaten and robbed of their lunch money." These are just samples of headlines I see every day in our local paper. Is it any wonder that people think something has to be done about crime in the streets?

2. Holding Attention   Beginning an essay with an abrupt or argumentative statement of your position may turn your reader off. For instance, if you were going to write a paper debating the relative merits of two political candidates, you would not want to begin by saying:

> I think Jim Williams, Patriotic Party candidate for city council, is a mentally unbalanced crook.

Even if this is what you want to tell your readers, it is a risky way to begin; you would appeal only to those who already agreed with you. A more gradual, controlled presentation of your opinion would be more likely to be read through by the undecided people whom you want to reach. You might instead try an opening like this:

> Although Jim Williams has built up quite a substantial following in his two years as dogcatcher, his 1972 conviction for embezzlement of city funds and his subsequent confinement to a state mental hospital raise serious doubts about his qualifications for a seat on the city council.

3. Stating the Controlling Idea   Besides attracting and holding your readers' attention, the introduction introduces the subject matter of the essay and indicates, through the controlling idea, what will be discussed. In Chapter 2, you remember, there were two main kinds of controlling ideas: *narrow*, in which you list the specific points of the discussion to follow, and *broad*, in which you set the limits of the discussion without actually stating its major points.

As you will also remember, the controlling idea usually comes at the end of the introductory paragraph. The introduction should gradually narrow the focus until it can lead into the controlling idea. You open with a few general remarks designed to interest your readers, proceed to more specific statements concerning the topic, and finally end by presenting the controlling idea.

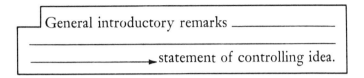

General introductory remarks ——————————
————————————————————
———————————————➤ statement of controlling idea.

In this opening paragraph notice how the writer follows this pattern, moving from the general to the specific:

> When I applied for admission to the University last year, I also applied for financial aid. Unfortunately, I was told at that time that all scholarships had already been awarded. I was advised to reapply for financial aid after my first semester. I would like to take this opportunity to do so, since my financial needs remain the same.

This introduction does not summarize the entire letter. It gives just enough information to orient readers, arouse their curiosity, and present a broad controlling idea effectively. You can get a general sense of the letter from this one paragraph; the introduction prepared you for the more detailed material to come in the body of the letter.

Remember:
A good introduction should:
1. Attract the readers' attention.
2. Hold the readers' attention and make them receptive to the writer's ideas.
3. Move gradually from general opening statements to a specific controlling idea.

Some Examples

All the introductions that follow are different in the

way they treat their subjects. While you can probably think of other approaches, these are the most common forms of introductory paragraphs:

1. Direct announcement
2. Quotation or dialogue
3. Anecdote
4. Definition
5. Refutation
6. Series of unrelated facts
7. Question

Keep in mind that different situations and purposes call for different introductory techniques; part of writing a good introduction is knowing when to select a particular strategy.

1. Direct Announcement   Often, beginning and experienced writers alike choose to open their essays with a straightforward announcement of the argument to follow. This "no frills" approach moves a reader directly and boldly into the core of the essay. The writer's approach may be gradual—moving point by point from general introductory remarks to a specific controlling idea—or it may be "head on," stating the major point to be discussed at once. The controlling idea may therefore appear at the end of the paragraph or in the very first sentence.

Midterms or final exams are not the best places for subtlety; they are ideal situations in which to use direct announcement. The following first paragraph introduces an answer to the exam question "Choose two recent Supreme Court rulings and show how they have affected law enforcement in this country."

> During the last twenty years, the Supreme Court has made many far-reaching decisions. The Warren Court in particular has been responsible for opinions that have significantly affected the rights of individuals accused of crimes. Several of these rulings have touched off debates among law enforcement

officials. The two most controversial decisions of the Warren Court have been reached in the Escobedo and Miranda cases.

The controlling idea is announced at the end of this introduction. The paragraphs to follow will be about "the two most controversial decisions of the Warren Court." Reasons, examples, and explanations will be presented in the body paragraphs.

A write-up of a scientific experiment also calls for direct announcement, because its object is to describe, as specifically as possible, the purpose of the inquiry. Here the "head on" approach is used.

This inquiry is to show that the rate at which you breathe is controlled in such a manner that under most conditions you are not aware of the changes in your breathing rate. This inquiry will also show the factors that influence breathing rate. These changes represent an adjustment to the body's respiratory needs. Also, it will show that people who regularly participate in sports have better control over their breathing habits than do nonathletic people.

Notice that in this no-nonsense format the controlling idea is presented in the first sentence. The rest of the introduction outlines the assumptions of the experiment and calls the readers' attention to the points to be proved.

Although the "direct announcement" introduction is straightforward, that doesn't mean it has to be dull. In this magazine article, the "head on" approach uses the built-in shock value of the word "botulism" to get attention.

Botulism—the very word strikes terror. And well it might, for this insidious form of food poisoning, usually caused by improper home canning, can para-

lyze in hours and kill agonizingly in days. On the rise
in recent years and threatening ever larger numbers
of people because of the great increase in home gar-
dening and canning, botulism is now playing its
deadly game by some curious new rules. (Liz Wick
Murphy, "The Case of the Homemade Poison,"
Good Housekeeping.)

The article is about the case of a two-year-old child
who contracted the disease from home-canned tomato juice. Each of the points considered in the opening paragraph is discussed in the article: the horrible
course of the disease, its recent increase, and its "curious new rules" (tomato juice, because of its high acid-
ity, had always been thought to be resistant to contamination). The essay is intended to shout a warning;
its bold opening, therefore, is an appropriate one.

EXERCISE 1

Using "direct announcement," write an introductory
paragraph on the topic "Should the Law Allow a Ter-
minally Ill Person to Take His/Her Own Life?"

2. Quotation or Dialogue   A short quotation, a bit
of dialogue, or even a particularly apt proverb or saying
related to your topic can be an effective opening. If
well chosen, the quotation should immediately attract
attention. Useful quotations may come from the newspapers: statistics, campaign promises, advertising slo-
gans, and even weather forecasts can all be used
effectively.

A personal experience essay on a death in the family,
written for an English composition course, begins this
way:

"You're the man of the house now," my uncle
told me. Two hours before, my father had been
taken ill on the job; within half an hour he had died
of an embolism. In those two hours nothing seemed

to have changed: my younger sisters were roller-skating outside, my mother was making coffee in the kitchen. But now I wasn't allowed to be a kid any more; suddenly, I was expected to grow up.

The essay need never refer to the writer's uncle again; the quotation is merely a springboard. The implied controlling idea is the fact that it's hard to grow up overnight; what the quotation does is to involve the readers in the situation immediately and plunge them into the action to follow.

An editorial from a student newspaper uses a quotation to involve the reader in the discussion.

"A newspaper should print news, not opinions." This statement seemed to be popular after the last provocative issue of the *Panacea*, which was roughly 43 percent opinion. It seemed, too, that an oversensitive student body prefers to read ambivalent and dull facts, rather than opinions that challenge the overall sentiments of this college community.

The opening quotation sums up student criticism of the last issue of the *Panacea*. By echoing their feelings, it draws readers of the paper into the essay. Then the paragraph presents a controlling idea that questions the quotation and actually does "challenge the sentiments of the college community."

EXERCISE 2   Beginning with a quotation or dialogue, write an opening paragraph for an essay on the topic "Discuss the Advantages and/or Disadvantages of Being the Oldest/Youngest/Middle/Only Child in the Family.

3. Anecdote   Another way to begin an essay is with a brief anecdote or story, perhaps drawn from personal experience or a recent event. This device involves the reader with the essay immediately.

In the following essay, the writer uses an anecdote to set the scene.

Here's the situation. Barbara Blair is a staff nurse on the three-to-eleven shift with three aides and three other nurses. Suddenly, out of the blue, Mrs. Adams confides in Barbara that she and the other aides are fed up with the lack of direction, the lack of respect, and the lack of cooperation they get from the nurses. She mentions particularly the different expectations Marie Jones, the assistant head nurse, and Judy Smith, the charge nurse on Marie's day off, have for the aides. She also deplores the lack of respect the nurses show by ignoring the aides' recommendations and refusing to help answer patients' bells. Barbara knows the complaints are justified and she promises to help. But what can she do? (Lory Wiley, "Tips for the Timid; or, How Can One Little Nurse Hope to Change the Rules?" *Nursing 76*.)

The above introduction is the first paragraph of a rather long article from a nursing journal. By using an anecdote to establish the situation, the author immediately interests her readers and moves them toward the controlling idea, stated as a question, in the final sentence. The rest of the article will attempt to answer the question raised in this first paragraph by suggesting ways in which nurses can effect change on the job.

Personal-experience essays often begin with an anecdote. In the opening paragraph, below, from an essay on anorexia nervosa (a psychological malady that leads its victims, usually teenaged girls, to starve themselves) a student writer uses an anecdote to arouse her readers' curiosity and involve them in her story.

The girl who waved to me had my cousin Sarah's red hair, but the rest of Sarah was gone. I had come to the train station to meet a normal, healthy 16 year old, but the Sarah who came toward me carrying a suitcase looked like a victim of a concentration camp. She could not have weighed more than 90 pounds—and she was 5'4" tall. "You look—different," I managed; "so thin—" "Oh no," Sarah interrupted, her gaunt face lighting up, "But wait till you see me after I lose another 5 pounds!" So began my introduction to anorexia nervosa.

EXERCISE 3   Beginning with a brief anecdote, write an opening paragraph for a paper discussing the question "Is There Too Much Violence in Hockey?"

4. **Definition**   If you plan to write an essay whose controlling idea involves a general, abstract, confusing, or obscure concept, the introductory paragraph must define it. Many concepts have more than one meaning, and you owe it to your readers to explain which one you have in mind. Or you may prefer to discuss several aspects of a topic. In this case, your reader should be advised of your intention.

A student essay on *Don Quixote*, a seventeenth-century Spanish picaresque novel, begins with a definition of the literary term *picaresque*.

A picaresque novel is one that has as its central figure a picaro, or adventurous vagabond, who wanders from one place to another. The novel is episodic, presenting each of the protagonist's adventures almost as a separate story. Such a novel is Cervantes' *Don Quixote*, whose hero is a romantic dreamer who struggles valiantly to conquer evil.

The following paragraphs will focus on *Don Quixote* as an example of the picaresque genre, providing examples of the most memorable episodes in the book as well as an overview of the hero's progress. By defining the essay's central concept early in her writing, the student author makes sure that her readers will be able to follow her essay.

Often an essay exam may require a definition as part of a larger answer. Sometimes, however, an exam or essay topic may ask for an *extended* definition. In that event, your answer's first paragraph should not attempt the complete definition—that's what the whole essay is to do—but rather set forth the aspects of it to be discussed. In this case, even a "dictionary definition" may be a useful introduction to the longer, more detailed treatment you will provide. Here is the first paragraph of a possible answer to the essay exam question "Compare and contrast Jeffersonian and Jacksonian democracy, discussing in your answer the strengths and weaknesses of each system." The paragraph uses a general definition to introduce the concept of democracy before narrowing to a controlling idea that states the kinds of democracy the essay will discuss.

Any discussion of Jacksonian and/or Jeffersonian democracy will only naturally begin with a basic understanding of democracy itself as it has developed in America. Democracy is many things to Americans: it is government in which the people rule, government by majority. To most of us, democracy also encompasses some measure of equal rights. To Thomas Jefferson and to Andrew Jackson, democracy meant both of these things, yet their concepts of a "democratic" government differed as their views of the American experience did.

EXERCISE 4

Write an introductory paragraph on the topic "Have You Ever Been Discriminated Against?" Begin your paragraph with a definition.

5. Refutation   The strategy of refutation involves disagreeing with a widely held assumption or belief. This creates interest because it is provocative; contradiction immediately introduces conflict.

The opening paragraph of an essay on sickle-cell

anemia, written by a student in a public-health seminar, uses the strategy of refutation.

> Sickle-cell anemia, a serious disease that mainly threatens blacks, has recently become the target of an extensive health campaign on both state and federal levels. This campaign has been received by the public with tremendous approval. It's about time, however, that the other side of the story was revealed. For, although the programs to test for and treat the disease have undoubtedly been undertaken with good intentions, they have had some decidedly negative effects.

This introduction offers a new interpretation of events: the writer suggests that, contrary to commonly held views, government programs to control and treat sickle-cell anemia have produced negative results.

The opening sentence announces the writer's intention to discuss the government's efforts to diagnose and treat sickle-cell anemia. The refutation begins in the third sentence, with the phrase "It's about time, however . . ." Words like *but* or *actually* can also signal refutation.

You can also begin a personal opinion paper with refutation. It is a natural choice for this student's course evaluation.

> All through the semester I have heard other students complaining about how unnecessarily difficult this physics course was. They resented the fact that Dr. Frank expected us to know not only the mathematical formulas but the theories behind them as well. Many students criticized him when he asked us to write a ten-page paper examining the scientific history of a great discovery in physics. They claimed that this type of assignment was a waste of time. But I disagree. This is the first science course

I have ever taken where I actually understood what I was doing.

Refutation is an excellent type of introduction to use, because it provides a ready-made frame for your discussion. By presenting the most obvious argument against your position in your opening paragraph, you give an edge to your controlling idea. Not only can you present your ideas, but you can also refute major criticism of them, all in the same essay. And not only does this technique make for a strong paper, but, by including both sides of the issue, it also adds greater depth to your discussion.

However, be sure that the opposing opinion you refute is a real one, and that you really meet it head on with your refutation. If the opposition is imaginary, something you made up only to knock down (what is sometimes called a "straw man"), your audience will suspect you of trickery; and if your refutation misses the point, your readers may award the "debate" to the opposition.

EXERCISE 5

Using the strategy of refutation, write an opening paragraph for a paper on the topic "Is It Better to Begin College Immediately after High School, or to Wait?"

6. Series of Unrelated Facts   One way to draw readers into a piece of writing is to make them curious about how the author will find common ground among a series of seemingly unrelated events or details. Journalists frequently use this technique.

In the following newspaper article, a series of events is introduced one by one. The final sentence ties the events together and provides the article's controlling idea. (In this article, what would be covered in one paragraph in a student essay is broken into four paragraphs. This is because the narrow newspaper columns make long paragraphs hard to read.)

LONDON, Dec. 6—The other night a 50-year-old man arrived at a Hertfordshire hospital complaining of chest pains. Refused admission, he drove to a hospital five miles away, where doctors discovered he had suffered not one but two mild heart attacks.

At about the same time a 66-year-old woman arrived at Hillingdon Hospital, Middlesex, with bleeding ulcers. After searching fruitlessly for someone to assist in the operating room, the surgeon on duty operated alone, barely saving the woman's life.

Later that evening an assistant manager of a pub in northwest London suffered head injuries in a road accident. Turned away at one hospital, the ambulance rushed to another two miles away. The man died.

These are illustrations, though extreme ones, of what has happened to the quality and efficiency of health care here in what may be the most serious crisis in the 28-year history of Britain's nationalized health system. (*New York Times.*)

This strategy is not exclusively journalistic, however; you may find occasion to use it in your writing. In the following personal-experience essay, for example, the student writer uses this approach.

Early in June, 1975, a man in my neighborhood was shot to death by a robber. Two days later a riot broke out. Late that month my brother's wife gave birth to my mother's first grandchild. My mother never saw her grandchild, for she had suffered a stroke and had been in a coma since April. She died in July. In August my sister received a full scholarship that enabled her to become the first member of my family to attend college. The horror and joy of the summer of '75 will always be part of me; they taught me the profoundest lesson of my life: human existence can be a living hell, but love and hope can make hell bearable.

At first, you were probably puzzled as to what the essay was going to be about. Your curiosity may have encouraged you to continue reading. The essay following this introduction does not necessarily have to deal with each of the seemingly unrelated occurrences. Although the writer could have discussed each one in turn in the body of his essay, he didn't; they were simply devices to get to the controlling idea in an interesting way.

Here, as in the previous example, a series of events or situations is introduced one by one. The final sentence ties the events together and provides the article's controlling idea.

EXERCISE 6   Using a series of unrelated facts to introduce your subject, write an opening paragraph for a paper on the topic "What Do You Think Is Your Worst Habit?"

7. **Question** Beginning an essay with a question, a series of questions, or even a riddle may be a particularly provocative strategy. The writer may answer the question, or leave it hanging; in either case, most readers will want to read on.

In the following book report, the writer uses a question to introduce his subject.

> What was it like to be a black man in the Deep South during the nineteen-fifties? John Howard Griffin answers this question in his fascinating book, *Black Like Me.* Griffin, a white writer, chemically turned his skin black and traveled throughout the rural areas and large cities of the South. *Black Like Me* convincingly illustrates the discrimination southern black people faced daily.

The arresting opening question creates immediate interest. Curious, the reader wants to learn the answer. The paragraph then identifies the book and states the report's controlling idea.

A question can also be used to strike an informal, almost conversational note. The following paragraph opens with a question which draws the reader immediately into the central concerns of the essay.

Ever had trouble calling a married woman friend because you didn't know her phone number or her husband's first name? In Israel and Switzerland, the names of both husband and wife appear in the telephone directories. And, if Assistant Attorney General William Griffin and Attorney Mary Skinner have their way, the state of Vermont will follow suit. (Suzanne Bailey, "Double Entry at Last," *Ms.*)

EXERCISE 7

Beginning with a question, write an introductory paragraph on the topic "Should the Government Compensate Homemakers for Housework?"

EXERCISE 8

The three paragraphs that follow introduce articles of various lengths in a newspaper. Each uses one—or a combination—of the strategies we have discussed. For each paragraph, identify the strategy, say how effective you think it is, and outline what the essay is likely to go on to say. In each case, consider whether another strategy might have worked better—and, if so, which one.

1. Portable electric sanders have probably done more to "liberate" the home craftsman and do-it-yourselfer from tedious hand labor than almost any other power tool. They permit the handyman or handywoman to effortlessly smooth and polish wood and plastic in a fraction of the time required for doing the same job by hand. However, as with any other tool, satisfactory results will only be achieved if the right type of machine is selected for specific jobs, and if the machine is properly handled. There are basically three types of electric sanders available for home use: disk sanders, finishing sanders and belt sanders. (Bernard Gladstone, "Handyman's Guide to Power Sanders," *New York Times.*)

2. Who served in the Vietnam War? Of the 234 draft eligible sons of members of Congress, only 26

went to Vietnam and only eight saw any combat. One of the eight was wounded; none was killed. Vice President Agnew's son served there but he came home o.k. Vice President Humphrey once called the Vietnam War "our great adventure," but none of his draft-age sons was in it. President Kennedy, who edged us into the war, had no draftable children. President Johnson, who heartily desired that America's soldiers bring home a coonskin for the wall, had no sons to give to his country's military service, nor did President Nixon, who once mused that the Vietnam War "may have been our finest hour." Outside official Washington, however, Americans were not so keen on the war and not so lucky; 56,869 were killed in Vietnam. (Review of C. D. B. Bryan's *Friendly Fire, New York Times Book Review.*)

3. Fourteen-year-old Saul Hansell of Detroit is finally getting his bar mitzvah trip to Israel and Europe this month—a year late. In Attleboro, Mass., Harold Blackburn, a store owner who took last year what he thought would be a last vacation before the economic collapse, now feels "an urge to spend more" on a bigger trip this summer. And in New York, Nancy Baxter, a 33-year-old publicist whose vacation last year consisted of a visit to her parents in Kansas City, this year says, "I feel rich," and is looking forward to spending $1,000 this summer on a three-week trip to Paris and London. Across the nation, Americans are dusting off road maps and resort brochures and preparing to take to the highways, skies and seas in what is shaping up as a boom travel summer after last year's recessionary slump. Their wanderlust rekindled by the resurgent economy, cut-rate tour packages and their own accumulated restlessness after a year or more of canceled trips and closer-to-home vacations, they are signing up for exotic and well-known holiday destinations with a fervor unseen since the 1973 fuel crisis gave

travel a bad name and sent the industry into a tail-spin. (Ralph Blumenthal, "More Americans Travel . . . , Longer Vacations Are Planned," *New York Times*.)

Choosing an Appropriate Introduction

Choosing an introduction is not a task that you should take lightly. The ease with which your introduction enables readers to grasp your controlling idea, the way it orients them or stimulates their interest, determines its effectiveness. The purpose of your essay, how familiar your audience is with your subject, and the occasion of your writing also should influence your choice of an introduction. A midterm or final exam might benefit from a direct announcement, while a personal narrative might best be started with an anecdote or a series of unrelated facts; an essay on Tay-Sachs disease to be read to your composition class could begin with a definition, while a short paper on the Farmer-Labor party for your political-science instructor could be introduced with a question. Whatever the case, remember that you should examine a number of factors when deciding what kind of introduction you will use to begin your essay.

Read over the following student illustration essay, written for a composition class, paying careful attention to its introductory paragraph. Write down what you think the strengths and weaknesses of its introduction are.

A Solution to Graffiti Problems

Direct
Announcement

There is no one complete method of solving the graffiti problem. Increased lighting of streets and buildings at night, limited sales of spray paint cans, and new graffiti-proof building materials can all help to decrease the graffiti problem. Graffiti removal is a costly process and all of these methods should be used to try and decrease the problem of graffiti.

Although increased lighting of streets and buildings may be an added expense, the long-term benefit of fewer graffiti will outweigh the initial lighting costs. Well-lighted areas are more easily policed than dark ones. To the graffiti artist, therefore, they are undesirable. Added lighting will not only decrease graffiti but all forms of vandalism, and it is therefore worth the extra cost.

Most graffiti are done with spray paint in portable cans. This type of graffiti is also the most difficult to remove. Limiting the sale of these cans through special taxes or other means would therefore decrease the most destructive type of graffiti vandalism. Moreover, many legislators are considering using the spray paint can taxes to clean up existing graffiti. Although the taxes are not yet in effect for aerosol paint cans, they should be since they could both reduce new graffiti and clean up old graffiti.

Finally, new building materials should be used to make graffiti removal less expensive. At present, materials such as concrete and brick require expensive sand-blasting techniques to remove spray paint graffiti. If the lower ten feet of all brick and concrete buildings were covered with vinyl or plastic, the cleanup would be much less expensive. These new materials would probably pay for themselves in a few years by decreasing cleanup costs.

Graffiti can be decreased by employing several preventive measures. These measures would pay for themselves in decreased cleanup costs and in one case actually generate money to pay for the cleanup. By using this combination of techniques, graffiti could be at least minimized, if not stopped altogether.

As you saw, the opening paragraph introduces its subject by direct announcement. Although this strategy works fairly well, it is rather dull. The paragraph does present the controlling idea in a clear and orderly way and even introduces the specific examples to be discussed, but it does not arouse much curiosity about the essay to follow. Would you have read on if you had found the piece in a magazine?

An alternative opening paragraph could be:

Question and
Series of
Unrelated Facts

> What do Cornbread, Cool Earl, and Rembrandt have in common? "Nothing," say the millions who are appalled at the notion of graffiti by the first two well-known Philadelphia graffiti "artists" whose work has defaced many city buildings. "Quite a bit," argue the defenders of this unusual kind of "folk art." While a vocal minority champions the spray paint "artists," concerned citizens are banding together to find a solution to problems created by such "creative expression."

This opening combines several of the major opening strategies. It opens with a puzzling question; it also presents a series of seemingly unrelated names that are linked by the controlling idea; and it uses refutation to dismiss one view before proceeding to state an opposing view. Note that the controlling idea is broad; the specific points to be discussed—the solutions themselves—are not mentioned.

Since understanding the term "graffiti" is crucial to a reader's understanding of this essay, another appropriate approach could be definition. In the following paragraph, an all-purpose dictionary definition is contrasted with a newer meaning of the word, a meaning that leads directly to the controlling idea.

> "Graffiti" is an Italian word that refers to words or phrases written on public sidewalks or buildings. Ancient examples of this "public writing" were found on the walls of the city of Pompeii

Definition

> when it was unearthed. Today the term often sig-
> nifies the spray-painted slogans that "decorate"
> urban schools, houses, and even subway cars.
> To some people—psychologists and sociologists for
> the most part—such graffiti are a valid and even
> artistic means of self-expression. To most people,
> however, graffiti represent an ever-increasing ur-
> ban problem calling for an immediate solution.

The definition, which establishes the writer's topic, is followed by refutation (the last sentence's "however" moves the paragraph from an argument for graffiti to the writer's own controlling idea that it is a problem).

Because so many prominent people have taken positions on graffiti, the strategy of opening with a quotation by an "expert" suits this particular topic quite well.

Quotation

> In a national symposium on graffiti, David Adams,
> noted art historian, stated: "Time was when 'Kil-
> roy was here' decorated many out-of-the-way
> places, but now it has been replaced by more exotic
> signatures, and the penciled comments have given
> way to spray-painted slogans." As Dr. Adams
> pointed out, once graffiti writing moved out of the
> rest rooms and onto the streets, it immediately be-
> came an object of concern among citizens trying to
> solve our urban problems. Elimination of this un-
> sightly blight presents a real problem.

Here, as in the preceding examples, we can't yet tell what the writer's specific suggestions will be. But the paragraph's last sentence introduces a broad controlling idea; we know that the essay will consider methods of eliminating graffiti.

EXERCISE 9   The introduction of the following illustration essay written for a composition class also uses the strategy of direct announcement. Again, this tactic makes for an adequate opening, but nothing really provocative or intriguing. The introduction needs more work to make the essay more appealing to its readers. Review the seven types of openings shown in this chapter, and then rewrite the introduction three times, each time using a different strategy. Try to make each introductory paragraph one that will immediately interest and involve the reader. Then note what you think the relative strengths and weaknesses of each strategy are, given the special requirements of this particular essay. The discussions of the introductions to the graffiti paper can be a guide for you.

Collecting Collectibles

Direct
Announcement

Stop! Don't throw away your used copies of *TV Guide* or *Redbook*. Some day they could be worth a fortune. During the past ten years, collecting as a source of pleasure and profit has increased markedly. Old Christmas cards, advertisements, restaurant menus, and magazines are being hoarded by an ever-growing number of collectors. Pinball machines, postcards, and matchbook covers illustrate just some of the items that are being collected seriously.

Once tucked away in arcades or bars, pinball machines are being gathered and proudly displayed by collectors. The world of the pinball *aficionado* is a fascinating array of color, lights, flippers, gongs, and bells. Names like *Riverboat, El Dorado, Lucky Aces, Pot O'Gold,* and *Flying Carpet* adorn some of the more popular machines. Bally, Williams, and D. Gottliebs manufactured most of these marvels of engineering and imagination and set standards that still guide the industry today. Interest in these collectibles has increased so rapidly that machines that could have been purchased a few years ago for under five hundred dollars now fetch thousands. Some avid collectors have been known to add whole wings to their homes just to accommodate their acquisitions.

Like pinball machines, postcards are being acquired eagerly by collectors. No longer the exclusive concern of children, this pastime is now big business. Deltiologists, as they like to call themselves, claim that their hobby is the fastest-growing in the world. London has at least twenty stores that cater to enthusiasts, and just last year New York hosted eight collectors' shows. Like other collectibles, postcards have rapidly risen in value. A late-nineteenth-century Art Nouveau postcard that sold for twenty-five dollars six years ago now costs over two hundred dollars. Many experts in this field see no end in sight for this increase in prices and recommend postcards as an ideal hedge against inflation.

People who collect matchbooks defend their pursuits as passionately as those who horde pinball machines or postcards. They say that matchbooks have been collected since 1816, when matches were invented, and before that, if you count tinder boxes. Matchbooks from famous hotels that are no longer in existence, from cruise ships that have been retired, and even from luxury airships are among the rarest and most sought-after items. Many collectors specialize in certain geographic areas. Some try to get matchbooks from all fifty states or from every major city in a state. Others expand their horizons and attempt to gather matchbooks from every country in the world. As with other collectibles, trading is brisk, and valued items bring high prices.

Pinball machines, postcards, and matchbooks do not begin to suggest the full range of collecting. Barbed wire, cigar boxes, baby-food containers, Coke bottles, and even tickets for Beatles and Rolling Stones concerts are sought by collectors. So if within you is the desire to accumulate things and the ability to recognize the value of someone else's junk, then this hobby could be for you. With a bit of money and a good deal of work, you too can join the ever-growing number of people who are devoting their lives to collecting.

6

The
Body
Paragraphs

Structure of the Body Paragraphs

In Chapter 3 we discussed how to structure an essay around the controlling idea. We pointed out that once you determine what your controlling idea will be, you should consult the material you generated by brainstorming or listing for three reasons or examples supporting it. These reasons or examples can be made into topic sentences for each of the supporting paragraphs that comprise the central portion of your essay. It is the role of these body paragraphs that this chapter is about.

1. **The Topic Sentence** The major job of the body paragraphs is to support your essay's controlling idea. They provide reasons, examples, or arguments that clarify, expand, or develop its implications. Usually, the controlling idea of an essay gives little detailed information. The support paragraphs provide the depth of discussion that a well-developed essay needs.

Each body paragraph has a topic sentence that states one aspect of the controlling idea. Like the controlling idea itself, these topic sentences may be general and need to be supported or clarified by concrete details, facts, or explanations. The detailed information in the body paragraphs enables readers to understand more fully what the essay is trying to say.

Body
Paragraph

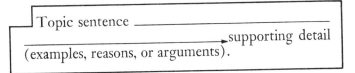

Topic sentence ——————————————
———————————————————➤supporting detail
(examples, reasons, or arguments).

Not only do topic sentences help you to structure an essay, but they also act as pointers, constantly referring back to the controlling idea, reminding your readers what the essay is about. Without a clear topic sentence, a support paragraph is likely to be fuzzy, out of focus —very much like an essay without a controlling idea. Reading such a paragraph or essay, you would be hard pressed to determine what it is about.

In the following paragraph, the topic sentence does not really relate to the rest of the paragraph. The student writer probably did not have any definite plan in mind when she started. The result is an accumulation of statements that seem to have no focus or direction.

<u>Shakespeare's Theater, the Globe, evolved from inn yards where actors originally performed plays.</u> Juliet stood on the balcony while Romeo spoke to her. Hamlet sat in front of the audience while speaking his soliloquy, "to be or not to be." Patrons would pay a penny to stand on the ground floor (hence the name "groundlings") and 2 pence to sit in a box above. Plays were generally well attended and greeted with enthusiasm when they pleased the audience and with jeers when they did not. Shakespeare's stage was also different from the picture-frame stage that we are used to. When considering any of his plays, these differences should be taken into account.

Even an excellent topic sentence could hardly draw so many unfocused elements together into one coherent paragraph. This topic sentence leads us to expect that the paragraph will demonstrate how Shakespeare's theater, the Globe, evolved from inn yards. Examples supporting this assertion would have accomplished this end. Instead, the writer goes on to discuss how much audience members paid to attend a play and where they sat. Had the writer decided in advance what she planned to discuss and constructed her topic sentence carefully to reflect her intention, she would not have gotten into this predicament. In contrast, the following paragraph has a strong unifying topic sentence right at the beginning.

> During World War II Vonnegut had an experience that changed his life even more. After being lost behind enemy lines, he was taken prisoner by the Germans. At one point in his imprisonment, he and other Americans were held captive in a slaughterhouse in Dresden while the city was bombed. The destruction of property and loss of life Vonnegut saw when he emerged from the slaughterhouse shocked him. Through much of his career, he tried to write a book about the bombing of Dresden; in *Slaughterhouse 5* he finally succeeded.

Body paragraphs with weak or inappropriate topic sentences need not always be completely rewritten. Sometimes, as with the following paragraph, just changing the topic sentence to conform to the material in the paragraph is all that is needed to draw the paragraph together.

> Recently scientists have been studying whales and porpoises. Not only did they find out that whales have a very complicated social structure, they also determined that it is possible that whales may actually talk to one another. Researchers now think that these huge mammals are so intelligent their brain capacity may even approach ours. The implications of this discovery are at once interesting and disturbing. For years now, we have been hunting and butchering a creature that very well could be our intellectual equal.

By changing the topic sentence to one that more clearly and definitely expresses the meaning of what is to follow, you can improve this paragraph. The old topic sentence seems to say that the paragraph will discuss whales *and* porpoises, but the paragraph then goes on to treat only whales. Also, the terms "recently" and "studying" are far too general to be interesting. A better topic sentence would be:

> For the past decade U.S. naval scientists have been experimenting with whales in an effort to determine their learning capacity.

EXERCISE 1

The following body paragraph has a topic sentence that does not relate to the ideas discussed in the paragraph. It can be improved in two ways: by rewriting the topic sentence, or by rewriting the rest of the paragraph. Revise the paragraph using both methods. Determine what must be rewritten by considering what the topic sentence indicates the paragraph should be about, and what the rest of the paragraph really says.

> Even though advertisements for alcoholic beverages portray drinking as romantic and exciting, it is clear that it is dangerous to the health and well-being of many young adults. Each year more than half of the fifty thousand automobile-related deaths are caused by people who, by legal definition, are too intoxicated to drive. The damage to property that drunk drivers cause runs into hundreds of millions of dollars. When you consider the time spent by doctors, firefighters, and police dealing with problem drinkers, the cost goes even higher. To make matters worse, insurance companies now claim that many home fires attributed to careless smoking actually involve alcohol.

Revision 1:

Supply a new topic sentence that conforms to the rest of the paragraph.

Each year more than half of the fifty-thousand automobile-related deaths are caused by people who, by legal definition, are too intoxicated to drive. The damage to property that drunk drivers cause runs into hundreds of millions of dollars. When you consider the time spent by doctors, fire-fighters, and police dealing with problem drinkers, the cost goes even higher. To make matters worse, insurance companies now claim that many home fires attributed to careless smoking actually involve alcohol.

Revision 2:   Rewrite the paragraph to make it conform to the topic sentence.

Even though advertisements for alcoholic beverages portray drinking as romantic and exciting, it is clear that it is dangerous to the health and well-being of many young adults.

2. Placement of the Topic Sentence   The three most common options for topic-sentence placement are:

   a. Topic sentence at the beginning.
   b. Topic sentence at the end.
   c. Topic sentence implied.

Topic Sentence at the Beginning. Placing a topic sentence at the beginning of a body paragraph can have a clear advantage: you let your readers know immediately what your body paragraph will be about. As the following paragraph illustrates, this placement orients your readers and prepares them for the discussion to follow.

> <u>The entire field of engineering is expected to experience faster than average growth in the next decade, with 46,500 openings for new engineers each year.</u> The Bureau of Labor Statistics says that the greatest number of job openings will be for electrical, industrial, civil, mechanical, and aerospace engineers. By field, growth is expected to be particularly strong in energy-related areas, chemical and environmental engineering. According to a survey by The National Society of Professional Engineers, the top salaries, both for new graduates and for experienced engineers with management experience, now are in the field of petroleum engineering. Chemical engineering and mechanical engineering jobs are also offering premium pay to those fresh out of college. (Mary Tuthill, "Where the Jobs Are," *Nation's Business.*)

You should place your topic sentence at the beginning of your body paragraphs in papers where it is crucial that your readers grasp your meaning. Midterm and final exams are obvious choices, as are short essays and letters in which you are conveying facts and examples.

In addition to orienting your readers, topic sentences at the beginning of your paragraphs can act as guideposts throughout your essay. They can keep your readers on track and, by referring back to your controlling idea, they can remind your readers what your essay is about. This repetition makes your essay easier to read and, for that reason, more enjoyable to your readers. The following outline shows how this repetition can work:

¶1 Controlling idea: Many Americans have trouble understanding the Moslem religion.

¶2 Topic sentence: The first problem Americans have with Islam is that
                         it does not separate church and state.
¶3 Topic sentence: The second obstacle Americans face when trying to
                         understand the Moslem religion is its demand for
                         absolute faith from its adherents.
¶4 Topic sentence: Finally, Americans have difficulty understanding the
                         strict regimen the believers of Islam must follow.
¶5 Restatement of the   It is a mistake, then, to think of Islam as a religion
   controlling idea: that is like the ones with which we are familiar.

Finally, topic sentences placed at the beginning of
body paragraphs can help *you* keep fixed on your subject. By referring to the topic sentences that you generate from your brainstorming material or your list, you
can make sure that you do not get sidetracked or bogged
down in irrelevancies. After finishing the first draft
of your essay, you should make a point of making sure
that your topic sentences are clearly stated, that they accurately sum up your paragraph, and that they reflect
your controlling idea. By using topic sentences in this
way you can provide a clear path for your readers
through your essay.

Topic Sentence at the End. Placing the topic sentence
at the end of your paragraph also has its advantages.
This technique keeps your audience in suspense
throughout the paragraph and maintains interest. Your
readers may be more likely to read on because, instead
of stating your main idea immediately, you have
gradually built up to it. Notice how the writer of the
following paragraph maintains interest by presenting
variant family structures before reaching the conclusion
that these are but a few of the many differences that
characterize family structures in different societies.

Families may be monogamous or polygamous—
there are systems where one man is entitled to several
wives and others where several husbands share one
wife. A society may recognize primarily the small
nuclear conjugal unit of husband and wife with their
immediate descendants or it may institutionalize the

large extended family linking several generations. . . .
Exchanges of goods and services may be based on
bride price, groom price, or on an equal ex-
change . . .; the choice of mate may be controlled by
parents or it may be left in large measure to the young
persons concerned. <u>These are but a few of the many
differences which characterize family structures in
variant societies.</u> (From Lewis Coser, *Sociology
through Literature*, Englewood Cliffs, N.J.: Prentice-
Hall, 1963.)

Placing your topic sentence at the end of a body
paragraph also forces readers to follow your chain of
reasoning as they read. Controversial issues, points
about which there will be debate, are best presented to
an audience in this way. By taking your readers through
your argument one step at a time, you are likely to convince them that the conclusion you reach is well considered and logical. A controversial conclusion at the
beginning of your paragraph could cause readers to
dismiss your points as unreasonable before they even
consider them. The following body paragraph from a
student essay discussing cruelty to domestic farm
animals follows this pattern of organization. By placing
his topic sentence at the end of the paragraph, the
student writer maintains reader interest and convin-
cingly presents his conclusion to his audience.

In many farms, a cage twenty inches by eighteen
inches (the size of an average college newspaper
page) is used to house four to five egg-laying hens.
Birds may live in this confined condition for between
a year and eighteen months. Artificial lighting, cli-
mate control, and drugs are used to squeeze the most
eggs out of each bird. Because conditions are so
cramped birds often get frustrated and viciously peck
one another. To offset any damage farmers often cut
the hens' beaks off. <u>These are just a few examples of
practices common in corporate farms all across the
country.</u>

The work-study student who wrote the following paragraph in a memo criticizing the operating procedures at a utility company places the topic sentence in the same way. By presenting the facts first, the writer prepares her audience to accept her conclusion.

Ten telephones, model number 50632, are presently in use in our office. The standard procedure is to handle incoming calls on a first come first served basis. There is little effort made to deal with calls according to need. In the past, operators have spent time with trivial matters while emergencies waited on hold. With the increase March 1 in our service area to include the Greentree district, we can expect this situation to get worse. <u>Now is the time to establish a system that will effectively deal with calls on a priority basis.</u>

Topic Sentence Implied. At times you might want to omit a topic sentence altogether. In some paragraphs—especially descriptive and narrative paragraphs—stating your main idea explicitly might seem forced and stiff. Many times a dominant impression or a series of facts or examples can effectively convey your meaning. The following paragraph is a thumbnail sketch of the inventor Thomas Alva Edison. Because the writer wants the readers to draw their own conclusion, he presents his paragraph without stating the obvious fact that Edison was a many-faceted individual.

He was a scruffy Midwestern kid who went to work on the railroad at the age of 12 but could never hold a job. He was brilliant and obtuse, charming and irascible, profane and profound. He hated cigarettes but chewed tobacco incessantly and smoked 20 cigars a day. He was a millionaire in his 30's but couldn't handle money, and it trickled through his fingers. He was a fascinating, frustrating, cantankerous maverick to whom few people who flick light switches on and off, by the hundreds of millions, give a thought. They pay their light bills but never consider their unpayable debt to the man who made possible, a century ago, their power and switches and incandescent bulbs, as well as the myriad other appliances of everyday life. (Robert Conot, "One Candle-Power Glow for a Century," *Smithsonian* September 1979.)

Whether you place your topic sentence at the beginning or end of your body paragraphs or whether you omit it altogether depends upon your purpose, occasion, and audience. If you have doubts about how to structure your body paragraphs, err on the side of clarity and put your topic sentence at the beginning. During the writing phase of your work—and especially when revising—remember to examine your topic sentences for placement, clarity, and function, to be sure that your body paragraphs contribute to the overall readability of your essay.

EXERCISE 2

Underline the topic sentences in the paragraphs below. Be able to discuss the reasons for placement of the topic sentence. If the topic sentence is implied, write a topic sentence that reflects the central idea of the pargaraph.

a. The Earl of Shaftesbury, the violent Whig who nearly toppled Charles II from his throne by exploiting the hysteria of the Popish Plot in 1678–1679, believed absolutely in astrology. John Locke, the naturalist philosopher, lived in his household, but made no impression it would seem on this aspect of Shaftesbury's beliefs. A Dutch doctor who dabbled in the occult had cast his horoscope and so, Shaftesbury thought, foretold all that would happen to him. Nor was Shaftesbury an isolated crank. The great German general, Wallenstein, who dominated the Thirty Years' War, took no action, military or political, without consulting the stars, and no one thought him either eccentric or pagan. (From J. H. Plumb, *In Light of History*, 1968.)

b. Animals seem to have an instinct for performing death alone, hidden. Even the largest, most conspicuous ones find ways to conceal themselves in time. If an elephant missteps and dies in an open place, the herd will carry the body from place to place, finally putting it down in some inexplicably suitable location. When elephants encounter a skeleton of an elephant out in the open, they methodically take up each of the bones and distribute them, in a ponderous ceremony, over neighboring acres. (From Lewis Thomas, "Death in the Open," in *The Lives of a Cell.*)

c. These sprays, dusts, and aerosols are now applied almost universally to farms, gardens, forests, and homes—nonselective chemicals that have the power to kill every insect, the "good" and the "bad," to still the song of the birds and the leaping of fish in the streams, to coat the leaves with a deadly film, and to linger in the soil—all this though the intended target may be only a few weeds or insects. Can anyone believe it is possible to lay down such a barrage of poisons on the surface of the earth without making it unfit for all life? (From Rachel Carson, *Silent Spring.*)

3. Development   Many writers have a great deal of trouble writing well-developed body paragraphs. They often write several short support paragraphs, each consisting of a series of generalities. Such writing is usually unconvincing and dull. Often, all that is needed to expand these undeveloped sentences into solid, effective support paragraphs is a bit of rewriting to add concrete detail. For example, here is a body paragraph taken from a student essay:

I had never seen anything like it before. The devastation was horrible. The tornado had cut a path of destruction through the town. It reminded me of pictures I had seen of bombed cities. Almost nothing had been left standing.

The writer of this paragraph wants to tell its readers of his impressions immediately after a tornado. The result, however, is a flat statement composed of familiar generalizations; anyone could have written it. Experienced writers know that it is one thing to tell a reader you were horrified, and quite a different thing to make the reader experience the dread you felt. The first requires only a simple statement: "I had never seen anything like it before," or "I couldn't believe my eyes." But to achieve the second, you must give your readers the details that will make them "see" what you saw, feel what you felt. The above paragraph does not do this. The writer has left out all the vivid specifics. Of course, he does tell you that "the tornado had cut a path of destruction through the town." But see how much more effective it is to *describe* that path of destruction for you.

<u>Although from four miles away I had seen the funnel cut through my home town, I was not prepared for the scene that stretched before me.</u> The tornado had cut a jagged line a hundred yards wide and a mile and a half long through the town. All along its path lay the twisted hulks of automobiles and the unrecognizable rubble of what once had been houses. Occasionally, as if to emphasize its capriciousness, the storm had left a single chimney or trailer untouched in the midst of broken brick, shattered wood, and convoluted metal.

Choosing specific, concrete details over vague, abstract language can make the difference between strong body paragraphs and weak ones. (The difference between concrete and abstract language is dealt with more fully in Section IV, "The Words.") The two paragraphs about the tornado, set side by side, reveal the difference:

Vague	Specific
1. I had never seen anything like it before.	1. Although from four miles away I had seen the funnel cut through my home town, I was not prepared for the scene that stretched before me.
2. The tornado had cut a path of destruction through the town.	2. The tornado had cut a jagged line a hundred yards wide and a mile and a half long through the town.
3. It reminded me of pictures I had seen of bombed cities.	3. All along its path lay the twisted hulks of automobiles and the unrecognizable rubble of what once had been houses.
4. Almost nothing had been left standing.	4. Occasionally, as if to emphasize its capriciousness, the storm had left a single chimney or trailer untouched in the midst of broken brick, shattered wood, and convoluted metal.

Adequate support is especially important in persuasive essays. When you are making a point in a short paper or in a final exam, you should supply enough important facts, details, reasons, examples, or helpful definitions to support your argument. Without adequate support, the body paragraphs of your paper will be vague and unconvincing. The following body paragraph illustrates this point.

Like Langston Hughes, Jean Toomer went to America for his subject matter. In his book *Cane* he examined the nature of black identity. He felt that in order to come to terms with the present, blacks would have to understand the past.

The writer of this body paragraph from a short paper on the Harlem Renaissance presents a clear statement of purpose with his topic sentence. However, he does not go on to discuss it in enough detail. How, for instance, did Jean Toomer examine the nature of black identity in *Cane?* What kind of book was *Cane?* In what way were blacks to come to terms with their past? The answers to these questions are never supplied. A more complete body paragraph would provide more specific information.

Like Langston Hughes, Jean Toomer went to America for his subject matter. *Cane,* written in 1923, is a mixture of short stories, poetry, and vignettes that explore the nature of black identity. Toomer traces black roots back to the South. In Part I of *Cane* he portrays Southern black life and shows how it has become limited and sterile. In Part II Toomer follows the black migration to the North and examines a different kind of sterility. Here, in cities like Washington and Chicago, blacks lose their vitality and identities and become enslaved by convention. Finally, in Part III, Toomer returns to the South and finds an answer to the question of black identity. Carrie Kate stands for the resolution Toomer believed was possible. She is able to embrace Father John, who represents the slave past of the blacks. By doing so she affirms her ability to absorb the dying past and face the uncertain future.

This body paragraph contains a lot of information about *Cane* and about its major theme, the American black writer's search for identity. The specific references to the book not only develop the topic sentence, but support it as well.

There is no set formula to determine how much support is enough: "enough" is what your audience needs to understand your subject. Remember that most readers will approach your essay with a slightly skeptical attitude. In other words, they are saying, "Prove it to me," and it is up to you to do just that—with facts, examples, and details. Readers need to be given a full explanation of your points; you should not assume that what you are saying will be self-evident to your readers. Even those who know something about your subject will still need to understand your approach to it. In the long run, it is better to give a bit too much information than too little.

EXERCISE 3 Here is a paragraph whose language is too general to be evocative or convincing. It could be improved by adding more concrete visual detail and specific factual information. Rewrite it so it will be more effective.

Air conditioning has made a big difference in the way we live. [*In this country only? Is this only an upper-class phenomenon?*] Many once deserted areas are now heavily populated. [*What areas? Why?*] People's summer recreation habits have changed drastically. [*What kind of people? What did they do before air conditioning? What do they do now?*] Many businesses are now run more efficiently during the summer months. [*How do you explain this increased efficiency? What kinds of businesses are affected?*] The trouble is, some people are starting to take air conditioning for granted.

4. **Transition** The word "transition" literally means movement from one place to another. In writing, transition means moving from one sentence to another or one paragraph to another smoothly and without abrupt shifts in logic or subject. To accomplish this, a writer will sometimes use certain words or phrases that act as bridges to carry readers into a new sentence or paragraph. Without these transitional elements, an essay can be like a list, or at best a group of loosely connected statements. Transitional elements prepare for each new idea and relate each new statement to the last. Here is a list of a few useful transitional elements, arranged according to their functions in a sentence:

Time	Contrast	Cause and Effect
then	however	therefore
now	nevertheless	thus
next	yet	hence
first	even though	consequently
second	despite	so

General to Specific	Addition	Reference
in fact	also	the former
especially	too	the latter
for instance	furthermore	the following
for example	moreover	

Summary	Attitude
in summary	fortunately
to sum up	unfortunately
in conclusion	naturally
	in a sense

In addition to transitional words and phrases, certain techniques establish continuity between sentences or paragraphs.

1. Repeating words, ideas, key phrases, or even a pattern of word order from sentence to sentence can serve this function.

2. Answering a question or completing an idea that has been left incomplete can give an essay a smooth flow.

3. The careful use of pronouns such as "this," "these," or "them" can carry over ideas by referring back to the previous sentence. (But keep in mind that an essay saturated with transitional elements and techniques can be as confusing and tiresome to a reader as one in which they have been left out.)

Perhaps the best way to see how useful transitions are is to look at a paragraph in which they are absent.

When I first began attending college, I had no idea what I wanted to do with my life. I am an accounting major. I will probably go into business for myself as a tax accountant. I have a much better idea of my goals. Last year I didn't know what to do with my major. When I was a freshman, I didn't even know I'd be an accounting major. Three years can make a lot of difference in terms of a young woman's career plans.

The sentences in this passage do not flow smoothly into one another. Without some signals of their sequence and logic, the relationships among them are hard to determine. Even the most basic transitions can eliminate some of the choppiness and ambiguity.

When I first began attending college, I had no idea what I wanted to do with my life. [Now] I am an accounting major, [and I know that someday] I will probably go into business for myself as a tax accountant. [At the present time, then,] I have a much better idea of my goals. Last year, [however,] I didn't know what to do with my major. When I was a freshman, I didn't even know that I'd be an accounting major. [This shows that] three years can [certainly] make a lot of difference in terms of a young woman's career plans.

EXERCISE 4   The following body paragraph lacks proper transitions. Supply the phrases or words necessary to improve the flow.

Perhaps the starkest portrayal of life in a Russian forced labor camp occurs in Alexander Solzhenitsyn's short story "One Day in the Life of Ivan Denisovich." [Transition] Camp life was something to be survived a day at a time. [Transition] The wake-up gong sounded, and prisoners were given ten minutes to rise and line up outside. [Transition] Prisoners stood in line for an hour in temperatures of 42° below zero [Transition] They walked through the snow for an hour to get to their worksite, "The Socialist Life Town." [Transition] There was no shelter or heat. [Transition] Many prisoners died. [Transition] Denisovich persisted. [Transition] He represents the Russian spirit that cannot be suppressed even by a dictatorial regime.

There is as much need for transition between paragraphs as between sentences. There should be no abrupt jumps or shifts in thought as your readers progress from paragraph to paragraph in an essay. Transitions at the proper places can ease your readers' passage from sentence to sentence and from paragraph to paragraph.

How the Body Paragraphs Work in the Essay

Suppose that you are asked to write a short five-paragraph essay either prosecuting or defending a man accused of a particularly bizarre ax murder of five young schoolchildren. Facts are obviously extremely important in a court of law, so you must present evidence that is specific, detailed, and concrete. Moreover, a courtroom situation requires a logical presentation of these facts, so transitions are equally important.

Let's say you decide to *defend* the alleged murderer, Harvey Hemphill. Here are some facts you can use: his mild character makes him an unlikely criminal; he has an airtight alibi; and the evidence suggests someone else. (Unlike most attorneys, you will have to invent the supporting detail yourself.) As usual, your first paragraph should introduce the controlling idea; your final paragraph should restate it and sum up. It is up to the three body paragraphs to support Mr. Hemphill's innocence. In the following essay notice how topic sentences, focus, development, and transition work together to create clear, fluid body paragraphs.

Title

In Defense of Harvey Hemphill

Controlling
Idea

Harvey Hemphill stands before you accused of murder. On the surface, the prosecuting attorney's case appears to be a strong one. But after considering the evidence, you can readily see that this is not so. Consider, ladies and gentlemen of the jury, Mr. Hemphill's shyness, his convincing alibi, and the persuasive evidence pointing to a mysterious intruder. Can Mr. Hemphill actually be the guilty party?

Topic Sentence
[Transition]
    Fact→

[Transition]
    Fact→
[Transition]
    Fact→
[Transition]
    Fact→

Harvey Hemphill is clearly too timid to be a murderer. [For one thing,] his army records show that he is a coward, terrified of weapons, hand-to-hand combat, and the sight of blood. [Furthermore,] his wife divorced him because she complained he was never able to make decisions or take any action. [This passivity] has been mentioned by virtually all of Mr. Hemphill's acquaintances. [Besides,] Mr. Hemphill was known to be especially shy around children.

[Transition
between
Paragraphs]
Topic Sentence

[Transition]
    Fact→
[Transition]
    Fact→

[Transition]

[While it is plain to see that my client's temperament makes him a highly unlikely ax murderer,] there is a more convincing reason for you to find him not guilty: he has an alibi. [At the exact time of the murder,] he was in the Lime Café, in full view of dozens of patrons. Twenty-seven [of these customers,] all respected members of the community, are willing to testify in court to Mr. Hemphill's presence in the café. [As a result] of this convincing evidence, my client could not possibly be the ax murderer.

[Transition
between
Paragraphs]

Topic Sentence

Fact→
[Transition]

Fact→
[Transition]
Fact→

[Not only is Mr. Hemphill a mild-mannered gentleman whose presence in the Lime Café proves he could not possibly have been at the scene of the crime,] but new evidence suggests that a mysterious intruder could have committed the murder. Two police officers and Mayor O'Rourke witnessed a shadowy figure running near the scene of the crime soon after the murder. [Moreover,] several hardened criminals are known to have escaped from the penitentiary on the morning of the crime. [Most convincing, of course,] is the presence of an unknown person's footprints near the house where the murders were committed.

[Transition
between
Paragraphs]
Restatement
of Controlling
Idea

Consider these facts, [then,] ladies and gentlemen of the jury, as you weigh the evidence. The evidence clearly raises a reasonable doubt about Mr. Hemphill's guilt, and his character and alibi offer additional support for his innocence. When these points have been weighed, I am certain your verdict will be "not guilty."

In this essay, each of the topic sentences discusses one aspect of the essay's controlling idea. Notice how effectively these topic sentences work to focus the essay, keeping the audience in touch with the internal logic of the presentation. Each topic sentence gives one reason why Hemphill could not have committed the crime he stands accused of.

Pay special attention to how specific facts are used by the writer to develop her ideas. Without them, the paper would be just a series of general statements asserting Hemphill's innocence. In order to convince a reader or a jury, the writer develops her assertions by using specific supporting data.

Note also the order in which the writer arranges her body paragraphs. She is careful to place her most important point *last*. Otherwise, the rest of her points would appear insignificant by comparison.

What is most important about this essay, however, is that all the factors discussed in this chapter work together to form a unified, well-developed, clear, and logical exposition.

EXERCISE 5   Now suppose that you are to take the opposite view of Harvey Hemphill, and to characterize him as a vicious killer. You are in possession of different facts from those stated by the defense attorney: Hemphill is known to be a cruel sadist; circumstantial evidence indicates he is guilty; and eyewitnesses say he is the guilty party. (Again, invent such supporting detail as you need.) The opening paragraph sets forth these points; the concluding paragraph restates them or sums them up. The body paragraphs must establish Hemphill's guilt beyond a reasonable doubt.

In the following body paragraph, supply the missing supporting details. (Transitional devices are bracketed; explain how each link is accomplished.)

> [First of all,] people in these parts have known for years that Hemphill had the makings of a sadistic killer. His mother, [for instance,] tells of the time he _____
> _____
> _____ . His first-grade teacher [also] _____
> _____ . The men he worked with at the plant [cite the time] __
> _____ .
> It is obvious from [these statements] that Hemphill is capable of committing murder.

In the following paragraph, facts are provided. Supply the missing transitional elements, referring to part

4 of this chapter if necessary. You are not limited to one-word transitions, although you may feel a word is sufficient in some cases.

[   ], circumstantial evidence points to Hemphill as the killer. [
   ], his car, a distinctive 1954 Cadillac El Dorado, was seen parked at the scene of the crime.
[   ], his fingerprints are all over the murder weapon. [   ], a lock of his hair was found clenched in one of the victims' hands. With such damning evidence against him, can Hemphill still claim innocence?

Complete the following paragraph, supplying adequate transitional elements and factual detail.

Most convincing of all, of course, is the eyewitness account of Miss Sadie Peabody, Sunday school teacher and church organist.

Remember: Every body paragraph should have an appropriate topic sentence, specific detail, and smooth transitions.

Read the following student essay over carefully; then underline topic sentences, put brackets around transitions between paragraphs and between sentences, and draw arrows to indicate supporting facts or details. When you have finished labeling these devices, consider their effectiveness and evaluate the body paragraphs. How could they be improved?

The Demand for Economic Reform in the 1930s

Throughout the 1930s demands from all segments of society kept constant pressure on the government. The reaction of the Roosevelt administration, not only to the economic hardships of the Depression, but also to this social unrest, was a series of programs which were at first intended to be temporary, but eventually became more permanent. Within a few short years, Congress enacted legislation to create massive welfare programs, social security, the Civilian Conservation Corps, the Works Progress Administration, and many other projects. All of these programs were created in response to the demand for change which was coming from all parts of the economic and political spectrum.

Senator Huey Long, for example, advocated a Share Our Wealth program. This would have prevented any family in America from owning a fortune of more than five million dollars, or having an income greater than one million dollars a year. In addition, the U.S. government was to provide every family in America with a homestead worth five thousand dollars, or with five thousand dollars in cash. The cash would be expected to cover the cost of a home, a radio, a car, and some other conveniences.

Father Charles Coughlin, the "radio priest," also recommended change in the government's economic policies. He felt that all U.S. citizens willing and able to work should receive an annual salary from the government. He also believed important public resources should not be owned by private individuals, but should be nationalized.

Dr. Francis Townsend, author of the Townsend Plan, was another who advocated government allowances. He recommended that the government pay its citizens over 60 years old a monthly two-hundred-dollar pension. This pension was to be funded by levying a sales tax. To earn a right to receive the pension, the recipient had to agree to retire from all business and professional activity, and to spend each month's entire stipend in the United States.

Populist, socialist, and Communist groups also proposed programs to solve the nation's problems, and the government responded by creating programs of its own. First recovery, and, later, reconstruction, were the Roosevelt administration's priorities. Eventually, the social and political ferment arising from the Depression era hardships was met head on by Roosevelt's solutions to the nation's economic problems.

EXERCISE 7

The following skeleton of a student essay consists of an introduction, a conclusion, and the topic sentences for three descriptive body paragraphs. Fill in the necessary supporting facts, supplying transitions between sentences and between paragraphs where necessary.

Neglected Wonders

When people become accustomed to looking at something, they stop seeing it. Sometimes, the most common objects, things people glance at every day, are not really seen at all, and so we find ourselves unable to really describe items we are used to seeing. Even worse, when we stop seeing things, we stop appreciating them. And when we take something for granted, it loses all value and all beauty.

A penny is one of these neglected wonders: not just a coin, but a miniature work of art.

An ordinary coat hanger is actually a marvel of engineering.

A rocking chair is a design triumph as well as an emotional symbol.

We look at pennies, coat hangers, and rocking chairs nearly every day, but how often do we take the time to *see* them, to examine their features, to consider their eccentricities? Maybe, as people have forgotten how to see, description has become a lost art. Will we ever stop looking at houses and trees and people and start seeing proud chimneys and noticing a branch that needs a child to climb it and studying the geography of a wrinkled face?

CHAPTER 7

The Concluding Paragraph

What It Does

Many books, movies, and speeches have achieved lasting fame because of their final lines. A conclusion has the power to draw together and clarify everything that has previously been said. If it is skillfully and dramatically constructed, the conclusion can be not only a summing up that bears the weight of all that has gone before it, but also a strong, succinct message in its own right. The fairy tale's "and they all lived happily ever after" and Lincoln's powerful "government of the people, by the people, for the people shall not perish from the earth" are effective and memorable in themselves, and also make the works they conclude more memorable—even famous.

Of course, not every essay you write—or read—can end as neatly as a fairy tale or as forcefully as the Gettysburg Address. But the concluding paragraphs of your essays always deserve a lot of thought. Why work so long and so hard at composing a stimulating introduction and well-developed body paragraphs if your effect is to be weakened by your conclusion? From one point of view, the conclusion of your essay is its most important part. It is your last word on the subject, your last chance to make your point to your readers.

Many readers will judge your essays by their final paragraphs. First impressions may be best in judging people, but as far as essays are concerned, the final impression seems to be the most lasting. Thus, a weak, abrupt, or uninteresting ending can detract greatly from what would otherwise be a memorable essay. A strong concluding statement is essential. It should focus your readers' attention on the main points, and hold that attention as effectively as the introduction does.

What, then, do all writers want a conclusion to do? Primarily, it should sum up, give readers a sense of completeness or finality, and perhaps help convince them. A common way of achieving these ends is to restate, in other words, the essay's controlling idea. This repetition underscores the points the entire essay has made and presents them (sometimes actually listing them) for the readers' consideration one final time. Often this restatement appears in the first sentence or two of the conclusion.

You can then expand your discussion by making some general concluding remarks—perhaps ending with a strong emphatic statement as a climax. If you intend your last lines to be remembered, the concluding paragraph must prepare your readers for this climax so it will not seem to be too abrupt. Dramatic last lines are even more effective when introduced gradually. In general, the conclusion can be said to be shaped like this:

Restatement of controlling idea ⟶ general

concluding remarks ⟶ final statement.

This way of organizing a conclusion enables you to let your readers go gradually, and to complete the essay while still holding their interest. It is not a gimmick or an oversimplification, but a technique many professional writers use quite often. Notice how the writer of a magazine article on violence shapes his conclusion.

These, then, are the main types of violence that I see. By recognizing those types of violence we begin to get the whole question of violence into a much richer perspective than when we hear the Chief of Police deplore violence. Such a richer perspective is vitally necessary, because we cannot do anything about the violence in our society unless we can see it, and most of us do not see it very well. Conceptions and perceptions are closely dependent on one another, and perhaps having a better idea what violence is will enable us to recognize more readily the many sorts of violence that surround our lives. (Newton Garver, "Four Kinds of Violence," *The Nation*.)

You can use this technique in your own writing. The student who wrote the following conclusion to a short essay used it well.

From this point of view, family expectations, peer group pressure, and social conditioning can all be seen to play a part in establishing sex roles. Up until quite recently, these roles have been narrowly defined: boys played with trucks, girls played with dolls; boys grew up to be doctors, girls grew up to be nurses. But now social trends are beginning to change, and sex roles are no longer so well defined. Clearly, more research is needed in order to discover how far-reaching these changes actually are.

Writers of fiction, investigative reporters, speech writers, teachers who write textbooks, and other have in mind the same goals you have for concluding written pieces. However, the actual form of the ending will vary somewhat according to the purpose and length of the piece of writing. A one-paragraph ending may be sufficient for a short essay, but a longer term paper or a book may require a conclusion whose momentum takes several paragraphs to build. On the other hand, a one-line conclusion may be suitable for a short fable, or a one- or two-paragraph exam answer. The important thing to remember is to construct your con-

clusions only after carefully considering the demands
of the essay you are writing.

Some Examples

Six commonly used concluding strategies are:
1. Restatement
2. Chronological wind-up
3. Illustration
4. Prediction
5. Recommendation of a course of action
6. Quotation or dialogue

1. Restatement   This is the most familiar type of conclusion. The controlling idea is repeated in different
words, and the main points of the essay's argument
are reviewed or restated. A straightforward essay, whose
introductory paragraph is a direct announcement, will
end this way. Restatement has the advantage of reinforcing one last time all your major points. For this
reason, it is an excellent concluding strategy for an
essay which seeks to prove a point.

The following example, the conclusion of a student
essay on living conditions in Appalachia, uses the technique of restatement.

> It is clear from even a casual trip through much
> of Appalachia that this region presents a challenge
> to a social planner. But before any utopian schemes
> can be considered, basic needs must be met. The re-
> gion's main problems remain very basic ones: inade-
> quate housing, poor nutrition, and a lack of educa-
> tional facilities.

This paragraph restates all the main points of the
essay in the order in which they appeared: poor housing,
poor diet, and poor schools. While this listing adds to
the essay's directness, a similar effect could be achieved
through a summarizing phrase like "social and eco-

nomic deprivation" instead of the three specific points.

An answer to a question on an early childhood development midterm ends with a restatement of the student's major points.

If a day-care center offers trained personnel, a spacious and safe environment, and creatively designed equipment, it can be a positive influence on a child. As recent studies have shown, there is no reason why a well-run day-care facility cannot be as warm and as stimulating as the child's home. As working parents realize this, many are passing up the traditional baby-sitter and turning to day-care centers.

In this answer the student discusses the advantages of day-care centers. The conclusion very effectively restates all the points that have been made. This technique is especially important on a test, when you want to present a logical, convincing, and easy-to-follow answer.

2. Chronological Wind-up   When a piece of writing "tells a story," it is natural to have its final paragraph tie up all loose ends by ending with what happened last. Personal experience essays and stories narrated in the first person often use this method.

Sir Arthur Conan Doyle's fictional Dr. Watson, first-person narrator of Sherlock Holmes' adventures, concludes a story in this manner:

And that was how a great scandal threatened to affect the kingdom of Bohemia, and how the best plans of Mr. Sherlock Holmes were beaten by a woman's wit. He used to make merry over the cleverness of women, but I have not heard him do it of late. And when he speaks of Irene Adler, or when he refers to her photograph, it is always under the honourable title of *the* woman. ("A Scandal in Bohemia.")

Similarly, this student ends a personal experience essay with a chronological wind-up.

> The next few years of my life passed quickly, probably because I was so busy. In the space of three years I got my equivalency diploma and held down three jobs—in sales, in the restaurant business, and in a men's clothing store. I also hitchhiked around the country. When I came back from my trip, I decided to return to school, and that's how I wound up in this English class, taking the first step toward getting a college degree.

The last paragraph of this essay ties all the loose ends together, leaving no room for further development. The student completes the narrative by bringing us up to the present.

3. Illustration To make an abstract or general conclusion more concrete and specific, you may choose to follow a restatement of your controlling idea with one or more specific examples to illustrate it. A reference to a relevant news item can often serve this purpose.

A first-person essay that expresses the writer's beliefs or opinions can also benefit from the use of illustrations. In this case, the writer may conclude with examples that strike a personal note, as John Wayne does in the following concluding paragraph from a patriotic essay.

> Day after day in America, people enjoy the good life. It's solid and it's real. There's so much here it's easy to take it for granted and to become alarmed at the headlines that shout out disasters in bold print. Just remember that the bad news makes up less than 2 percent of our nation's activities. The other 98 percent—a man towing a stranger's car to a garage, a neighbor caring for a sick child, or a minister making a call to a dying parishioner in a driving rain—doesn't make the headlines because it won't sell papers. But "Good Things," we have them, here in America. (John Wayne, "The Good Things: Duke on America," *Saturday Evening Post*, September 1979.)

In academic situations, too, you can make your essays clearer by adding specific examples in the conclusion to illustrate the restatement of the controlling idea. A student in an economics class ended a paper with a series of concrete examples.

> Despite the price gouging of oil companies and the reluctance of the Congress to formulate a co-ordinated domestic energy policy, there are some signs of hope. One such sign is a government study that recommends four encouraging options. The first is to put into effect a small program with limited rationing of oil resources. The second approach is to undertake a large project with emphasis on lower energy use and finding more domestic energy sources. The third option would be an all-out war against the energy problem. This would involve exploitation of shale oil, and immediate exploration and development of off-shore oil reserves. The fourth and final course would be a balanced ecologically oriented program that would attempt to cut down American energy use. Certainly, these courses of action do not solve our country's energy problems, but they do show that the government is finally approaching the issue in a more organized, methodical fashion than it has in the past.

By stating the government agency's "four options," the writer places his abstract ideas about "signs of hope" in perspective.

4. Prediction   Writing designed to convince or persuade your readers may very naturally end with a prediction that takes the conclusion a step further than a summary. This type of conclusion does sum up the essay's main points, but it also enables the writer to make certain additional projections on the basis of those points.

An article that somewhat humorously decries discrimination against short people and proclaims their
natural superiority concludes with this prediction:

> I am not suggesting for a moment that we actively
> dispose of existing tall people or that we selectively
> breed for shortness. Many of my best friends are
> tall, and I will not be a party to sizism. I am merely
> noting that, evolution being what it is, tall people
> are not long for this world. When small is beautiful
> and less is more, nature will single out us small people
> and make sure that we grow (numerically) apace.
> People will start taking pride in the fact that their
> children are shorter than they are. Aunts will exclaim
> "How small Johnny is staying!" Before long, tall
> people will be taking such defensive lines as "Good
> things come in large packages." It will not happen
> tomorrow, but it will happen. Short people are the
> wavelet of the future. (Beth Luey, "Short Shrift,"
> *Newsweek*, February 27, 1978.)

Students often use predictions as conclusions for essays and essay examinations. After discussing a series of
facts on an economics exam, you might want to show
how those facts might affect the future: "If some re-
forms are not immediately instituted in the Social Security system, there might be no money left for those
of us who will be ready to collect our checks forty-
five years hence." You can see the same strategy used
in all kinds of writing from journal articles to student
essays.

A nursing student ended his paper for a public health
course with this prediction:

> Even though there has not been a case of smallpox
> in the United States for years, children should still
> be vaccinated against this disease. Despite the as-
> surances of many doctors to the contrary, some phy-
> sicians still recommend this course of action. As far
> as this vocal minority is concerned, it is extremely

likely that failure to immunize against smallpox could result in an outbreak of epidemic proportions just like the one that recently occurred in Somalia.

5. Recommendation of a Course of Action   When you feel you have convinced your readers, you may want to recommend action. Writers of business correspondence are especially aware of the advantages of ending their letters with an appeal for action. Advertisements plead, "Don't forget, before it's too late. Clip this coupon and send away now." In editorials or political speeches, the call for action is usually the writer's main purpose. In these and other kinds of persuasive writing, it can be psychologically very effective to conclude by appealing to the reader for action.

A recommended course of action is almost always a part of political writing. A notable example is the very effective final paragraph of Marx and Engels' *Communist Manifesto:*

> The Communists disdain to conceal their views and aims. They openly declare that their ends can be attained only by the forcible overthrow of all existing social conditions. Let the ruling class tremble at a Communist revolution. The proletarians have nothing to lose but their chains. They have a world to win.
>   Workingmen of all countries, unite!

Student writers also sometimes find occasion to recommend action. This paragraph concluded a student essay that discussed the harmful effects of food additives.

> Every month the Food and Drug Administration finds that another food additive has harmful effects on humans. BHA, BHT, MSG, and red dye #2 are only a few of the substances under suspicion. In spite of this, food processors seem reluctant to eliminate additives from their food. It seems as if the only way

we, the consumers, will be able to make our desires
felt is to stop buying food that contains artificial preservatives and flavor enhancers. It is time for us to
take an active part in determining what we eat.

The writers' use of "Let" in the first example and
"It is time" in the second is characteristic of this type
of concluding strategy.
Letters applying for a job also often conclude with
an appeal or a request for action. The ending may
combine a summary of the writer's qualifications with
a request for an interview.

Since I plan to make teaching my permanent career, I would be a diligent and dedicated worker. I
feel that both my job experience and my educational
background in teaching the handicapped uniquely
qualify me for this position. I can come to Boise for
an interview at any time that would be convenient
for you.

6. Quotation or Dialogue   As in the introduction,
quotation can lend authority to a conclusion. Quotations by well-known authors can sometimes not only
sum up your essay handsomely, but also enable you to
use their distinctive writing styles to add variety and
interest to your conclusion.

Professional writers and journalists use this strategy
a great deal. Harrison Salisbury uses a quotation to end
his essay "Print Journalism."

What is at stake was well said by Walter Lippmann
in the aftermath of the Eastland case: "The . . .
principle of the First Amendment was not adopted
in order to favor newspapermen and to make them
privileged characters. It was adopted because a free
society cannot exist without a free press. The First
Amendment imposes many duties upon newspaper-

men who enjoy the privileges of this freedom. One of the prime duties of free journalists is that they should, to the best of their abilities, preserve intact for those who come after them the freedom which the First Amendment guarantees." (*Playboy*.)

By using Walter Lippmann's statement, Salisbury sums up his ideas and adds clout to his argument.

Quotations can be put to good use in your own writing. This conclusion from a final exam answer uses the words of Kurtz, a character from Joseph Conrad's *Heart of Darkness*, to sum up.

In its tone and its theme, *Heart of Darkness* illustrates Conrad's mixed attitude toward colonialism. On the one hand, he felt that the ideal represented by colonialism was good and noble. On the other hand, Conrad could not ignore the evils and abuses being committed by Europeans in Africa, evils best expressed by Kurtz in his final comment, "The Horror! The Horror!"

Choosing the Best Conclusion

As with introductions, it is your purpose and occasion that determine what kind of conclusion you should use. In midterm or final exams, in technical reports—in any paper in which your primary aim is to present information—a direct restatement or summary of your controlling idea may be your best strategy. Personal narratives, journal entries, and short stories can be effectively concluded with a chronological wind-up. Papers in which you try to convince your readers that a point you are making is valid can be ended using illustration, prediction, recommendation of a course of action, or a quotation.

The following student comparison-contrast essay

was written for a literature class. Take special note of how its conclusion works. Keep in mind that the student writer is trying to convince his readers that fairy-tale elements play an important role in the story.

Fairy Tale Elements
in "The Rocking Horse Winner"

D. H. Lawrence's short story "The Rocking Horse Winner" is clearly not a fairy tale but a modern psychological tale of a young boy trying desperately —and unsuccessfully—to please his mother. Its stylistic subtleties, unanswered questions, and psychological complexities set it apart from the conventional fairy tale. Unlike a fairy tale, it offers rational explanations for its fantastic events and it lacks a clear sense of good and evil; the adults in the story aren't evil, just weak and greedy—victims of extenuating circumstances. Finally, the story is unlike most familiar fairy tales in that it lacks the conventional happy ending. Despite these differences, however, the story does contain elements of the fairy tale that deserve to be explored.

In terms of structure and style, "The Rocking Horse Winner" and fairy tales share some striking resemblances. The story's plot, for instance, has a strong narrative line and seems throughout to be moving toward a conclusion that is somehow inevitable: the boy Paul, riding his toy rocking horse with such desperate hysteria, seems doomed from the start. The rhythmic style, with its frequent use of coordinating conjunctions, is also commonly found in fairy tales. The story's first three sentences are an excellent example: "There was a woman who was beautiful, who started with all the advantages, yet she had no luck. She married for love, and the love turned to dust. She had bonny children, yet she felt they had been thrust upon her, and she could not love them."

The frequent repetition of words and motifs is also

reminiscent of fairy tales. Over and over again the house seems to whisper, "There must be more money! There must be more money!" Over and over again the boy rides his horse to predict the winners of the major horse races, and over and over again he places large sums of money (which grow larger and larger as the story progresses) on the horses he believes will win. Over and over again the concept of luck—what it is, what it can do, what it means to be without it— is stressed.

Finally, the story shares with fairy tales its strong undercurrent of the supernatural, its sense of magic. While the events of the story are rooted in the real world and all seemingly magical events have clear logical (or psychological) explanations, the feeling of the supernatural persists. The boy's communication with his rocking horse and his ability to predict the winning horses with uncanny skill give the story a magical quality.

Restatement

> These elements, then—style and structure, repetition of words and motifs, and a sense of the supernatural—give "The Rocking Horse Winner" its parallels with the fairy tale. Such a comparison is by no means the only way to approach the story, of course. Still, it provides a new perspective for the reader to apply to a familiar story, and it can perhaps suggest new insights to the literary critic as well.

The ending, a simple but comprehensive restatement of the essay's broad controlling idea, serves to remind the reader of the elements that most clearly support the idea of a relationship between the story and a fairy tale. Its biggest strength is its clarity, which would make it particularly effective if this essay were part of an exam. Other options, however, are also possible. One alternative is to close with a quotation from the story.

Quotation

> As the story builds to a climax, the relationship between "The Rocking Horse Winner" and a fairy tale fades away. As Paul lies on his deathbed it is clear that good will not triumph over evil, that no rescuer will come to save the boy. The ending is neither pat nor hopeful: at his death the boy's uncle tells Paul's mother, "Poor devil, poor devil, he's best gone out of a life where he rides his rocking horse to find a winner."

By quoting a crucial bit of dialogue, the writer helps convince his readers that his assertion—that the ending is "neither pat nor hopeful"—is valid. In addition, he conveys the flavor of the story and its ending to the audience.

Another way of focusing on the story's final events is to summarize them and comment on their significance.

Chronological Wind-up

> In Lawrence's story, however, the magic ends. In one of his mad rides young Paul becomes delirious, his eyes blazing and his voice unnatural. He lapses into a coma, and several days later he dies. Despite the fairy-tale quality of "The Rocking Horse Winner," no one in the story lives happily ever after.

Here, the writer effectively sums up the story's final moments, without using dialogue, and ties them in with the essay's central point.

Another option is to use illustration. In the following conclusion, by showing a few specific parallels between the Lawrence story and "Cinderella," the writer is able to illustrate the essay's controlling idea and make it more concrete.

Illustration

In many ways Lawrence's story is like the fairy tales many young children read. In "Cinderella," for instance, a well-behaved child is treated cruelly by uncaring adults and helped by sympathetic animals. Like Cinderella, Paul is extraordinarily good, anxious to please, and yet unable to satisfy the demands of adults. He, too, is "helped" by an "animal"—his toy rocking horse. But here the resemblance between the two characters ends; "The Rocking Horse Winner" is no Cinderella story.

EXERCISE 1

Now that you have read the original essay and three possible alternative ways to conclude it, decide which conclusion seems to work best. Be prepared to discuss why you made the choice you did.

EXERCISE 2

The following essay on two of baseball's greats does a competent job of comparing and contrasting Babe Ruth and Hank Aaron. The concluding paragraph is a straightforward restatement of the essay's controlling idea: that both Ruth and Aaron, despite basic differences in style and personality, shared certain enviable athletic accomplishments.

Two Great Men

Baseball is one of America's finest pastimes, and Americans have always shown a great interest in this sport. Whenever people talk about baseball, one of the most exciting facets of the game, the home run, is always mentioned in the conversation. And when this part of the game is mentioned, two players' names always come to mind. These players are Babe Ruth and Hank Aaron, the greatest home run hitters in the history of the game.

Babe Ruth, known as "Mr. Baseball," is probably the most popular figure in the sport. He started his career as a pitcher who could swing a powerful bat, and this ability as a batter caused Babe to be converted into an outfielder. Eventually, he developed into the game's most feared home run hitter, leading the league in home runs in ten seasons and tying for the title in two. One season, Babe hit 60 home runs; in his lifetime, he hit 714. Sometimes, before a pitch, he would point his bat toward the seats in the outfield and then drill that pitch almost to the spot he had predicted. Babe became a legend, and many people thought his career home run count would never be surpassed.

In 1974 Babe's career home run record was broken by Hank Aaron. Hank, an outfielder, who was always a powerful hitter during his career, was not as well known a figure as Ruth even though he had been quietly replacing Babe as the game's most feared home run hitter. For one thing, he didn't play in the big city so he didn't get the publicity Ruth got. For another, the most home runs he hit during one season was 47. And Aaron would never do Ruth's canny trick of predicting home runs, because Hank was not flamboyant like Ruth. Like Ruth, however, Aaron led the league in home runs during several seasons and Aaron too became a legend in his own time.

Restatement

> Babe Ruth and Hank Aaron are both American heroes. These two players have made almost the same accomplishments on their roads to success even though their personalities are quite different. They have contributed greatly to the success of baseball.

While the conclusion does leave the reader with a sense of completeness, it is neither dramatic nor memorable. Write three of the five possible alternatives to this restatement conclusion. Again, consider the relative strengths and weaknesses of each strategy.

CHAPTER 8

Revising
Your
Paragraphs

Once you understand how an essay is organized, the chances are all your essays will have an introduction, a body, and a conclusion. Considering how effective these parts are in your essay becomes your next concern. The rough draft that appears here was submitted to a composition instructor and discussed during conference. While the essay is organized well, it is not as effective as it could be. After consulting the following checklist, the student began to revise his paper.

The Paragraphs

Does your introduction:
> Arouse interest?
> Adequately introduce the subject?
> Smoothly lead to the controlling idea?

Do your body paragraphs:
> Have topic sentences?
> Have supporting details?
> Include adequate transitions?

Does your conclusion:
> Restate the controlling idea?
> Contain general concluding remarks?
> Have a final closing statement?

Comments

Title could be more descriptive.

Your introduction is clear and to the point, but it could arouse more interest.

Rough Draft

Women and Sports

Women should be allowed to compete in athletic events along with men. It is time that American high schools stopped discriminating against women and gave them the same athletic benefits they do men.

Many female athletes receive inadequate training and coaching. It seems that not preparing females in a manner equal with men is discriminatory.

Each of your body paragraphs has only two sentences. Can you develop them more by adding details?

In many sports, females can easily compete with men. In these sports there is no reason why women should be prevented from playing.

Research has shown that a great number of women have a strong desire to be on co-ed teams. The desire to excel in athletics and to play to win is not limited to men.

Incomplete conclusion. While you do restate your controlling idea, you do not end effectively.

Women should no longer be prevented from competing with men in high school sports.

While I can see that you know how to organize an essay into introductory, body, and concluding paragraphs, you really need to develop your paragraphs further. Although your opening paragraph does introduce your essay and present your controlling idea, it is not a very interesting paragraph. Your body paragraphs do begin with topic sentences, but you don't go on to support those statements. More detail, and more specific examples, would do a lot to improve this section. Also, your conclusion is weak; it sounds as if you were in a hurry to finish up. A few concluding remarks and a strong closing statement would really help.

Revision 1

Title still needs work.

Women and High School Sports

Would anyone believe that twenty years after the Supreme Court outlawed discrimination in public schools, cases of overt segregation occur there daily? At present, in American high schools, women are not allowed to compete in athletic events with men. It is time that high schools stopped discriminating against women and gave them the same athletic benefits men have.

Introduction much better.

This body paragraph is really improved, but you could use a statement linking the topic sentence to the controlling idea.

Women receive inadequate athletic training and coaching. Recent reports have shown that women's athletic programs in high school receive about one-fifth the funding of men's programs. Not only does this stifle the athletic development of women, but it also clearly violates the intent of the Thirteenth and Fourteenth amendments.

This paragraph is weak—still not enough detail.

In many sports, women can easily compete with men. There is no real reason why, in most schools, women cannot join the tennis team. Women should not be prevented from playing.

Effective paragraph. Just one more sentence is needed at the end, to close it off or draw a conclusion.

Research has shown that a great number of women have a strong desire to play on co-ed teams. In cases where women have been allowed to join all-male teams, they have performed well. Opposition to them has come not from their teammates but from parents or school board members.

Conclusion is still pretty abrupt, and, compared to the rest of the essay, not very interesting.

Women should no longer be prevented from competing with men in high school sports. This certainly is a goal worth fighting for.

This draft is certainly better than the first one! You still need more detail, though, and some transitional phrases between sentences, and between paragraphs. Your conclusion needs life—try again.

Revision 2

Women's Participation in High School Sports

Would anyone believe that twenty years after the Supreme Court outlawed discrimination in public schools, cases of overt discrimination occur there daily? At present, in American high schools, women are not allowed to compete in athletic events with men. It is time that high schools stopped discriminating against women and gave them the same athletic benefits men have.

Nice link to controlling idea.

In most high schools, women receive inadequate training and coaching. Recent reports have shown that women's athletic programs in high school receive about one-fifth the funding of men's programs. Not only does this stifle the athletic development of women, but it also clearly violates the intent of the Thirteenth and Fourteenth amendments.

In many sports, women can easily compete with men. There is no real reason why, in most schools,

Good point!

women cannot, for example, join the tennis team. This is not a contact sport, and it depends on skill rather than strength. Women should not be prevented from playing any sport for which they can qualify.

Research has shown that a great number of women have a strong desire to play on co-ed teams. In cases where women have been allowed to join all-male teams, they have performed well. Opposition to them has come not from their teammates but from parents or school board members. It seems that if there were a referendum among students, all sex barriers would be dropped from high school athletics.

This paragraph is much stronger, and really does a lot for your essay.

Rules keeping women out of male high school athletics should be treated just like all laws or "gentlemen's agreements" that discriminate against others. Perhaps with the adoption of the ERA, this antiquated way of thinking will be eliminated. But until then, men and women who believe in equality will continue to fight for justice.

EXERCISE

Do you agree with all the changes this student made? Are there some you would not have made? Are there parts of the finished essay that still need revision? How would you revise them?

THE SENTENCES

By now you have a good idea of how to plan and structure your essays. You should next begin to concentrate on the way you form your sentences and the way you relate them to other sentences within a paragraph.

Your sentences should be grammatically complete, of course, but that is only the beginning of good writing. Like your essays and paragraphs, your sentences should communicate your ideas as clearly as possible; and, to keep your readers' interest, they should be varied in structure. If they are awkward, or padded with meaningless phrases, they will be difficult to understand. And if your sentences all begin with the same word and have the same basic structure, they will bore your readers the way a long, monotonous drive on a turnpike does.

By improving and varying your sentence style, you will not only write more effective sentences, but clearer, more interesting essays too.

CHAPTER 9

Sentence Patterns

Defining the Sentence

There are many ways you could try to define a sentence. You could say that a sentence is a group of words that expresses a complete thought. (But the same thing could be said of a book!) You could also say that a sentence is a group of words that includes a *subject* and a *predicate*. (But what are subjects and predicates?) You could even say a sentence is a unit of writing that begins with a capital letter and ends with a period. (But how does this help?) All these statements describe a sentence, but none is very useful without further definitions and discussion. Perhaps it is most useful to think of sentences in two ways: as short, grammatically complete pieces of writing (we'll talk about grammatical completeness soon), but also as parts of longer, unified stretches of writing—paragraphs and essays. Let's first look at sentences as sentences.

There are three basic types of sentences: simple, compound, and complex. Each of these basic patterns can be endlessly varied. To write sentences that are *clear*, you need to know how to construct each pattern; to write sentences that are *interesting*, you should know how to vary each pattern, and move from one pattern to another as you write.

The Patterns

1. The Simple Sentence In its most basic form, a simple sentence consists of a noun which is the *subject* and a verb which is the *predicate:*

<u>Twain</u> <u>wrote.</u>

The subject (Twain) is who or what the sentence is about. The predicate (wrote) contains a verb and states something about the subject.

The subject may be more than one word:

<u>Mark</u> <u>Twain</u> wrote.

There can actually be more than one subject:

<u>Mark Twain</u> and <u>Harriet Beecher Stowe</u> wrote.

The subject may also be preceded by an article:

<u>The</u> writers wrote.

or by a possessive pronoun:

<u>My</u> book is by Mark Twain.

or by an adjective:

<u>All</u> writers write.

The predicate may be in any tense and can also be more than one word:

The writers <u>should</u> <u>have</u> <u>written.</u>

A simple sentence may include descriptive words, or *modifiers*, like adjectives or adverbs:

The <u>two</u> writers should have written.
The two writers should have written <u>more.</u>

Finally, the simple sentence may include another word or group of words that provides additional information about the action the sentence describes. It may tell you when the action is being performed:

The two writers wrote <u>mainly in the nineteenth century.</u>

Or it may tell you who or what is being affected by the action:

Twain wrote <u>letters</u>.
Twain wrote letters <u>to William Dean Howells.</u>

These are only some of the many simple sentences that can be constructed using these parts of speech:

Article	(the)
Adjective	(two)
Noun (subject)	(Mark Twain, Harriet Beecher Stowe, writers)
Verb	(wrote, should have written)
Adverb	(more)
Noun (object)	(letters)
Phrase	(in the nineteenth century; to William Dean Howells)

EXERCISE 1

Construct five examples of the most basic *simple sentence*. Select one word from each word list for each sentence.

Subject	Predicate
Flem Snopes	scratched
George F. Babbitt	drinks
Natty Bumppo	apologized
Simon Legree	thought
Pudd'nhead Wilson	ran

1.

2.

3.

4.

5.

Now rewrite each of the above sentences, adding two of the following modifiers to each:

Adjective	Adverb
cruel	quickly
honest	sadly
evil	furiously
devious	clumsily
dedicated	quietly

1.

2.

3.

4.

5.

EXERCISE 2

Now construct five additional simple sentences, using the following words. Try to include both a phrase and a noun other than the subject in each sentence.

Example:

Nasty Natty Bumppo fiendishly kissed Eula Varner before the Civil War.
(This is nonsense, of course; just think of it as a way of practicing.)

Subject	Predicate
(Noun)	(Verb)
Flem Snopes	chased
George F. Babbitt	kissed
Natty Bumppo	whipped
Simon Legree	threatened
Pudd'nhead Wilson	captured

Descriptive Words

Adjective	Adverb
handsome	fiendishly
friendly	gracefully
nasty	triumphantly
embarrassed	passionately
nervous	childishly

Phrase	Noun
around the forest	Eula Varner
in the Zenith Athletic Club	Judge Driscoll
at the town meeting	Eunice Littlefield
before the Civil War	Hard-Heart
in front of the general store	Topsy

1.

2.

3.

4.

5.

EXERCISE 3

For more practice, construct five more *simple* sentences, using one of the nouns "attorney," "teacher," "secretary," "doctor," and "police officer." Combine each noun with an appropriate article and verb of your choice and then add your own descriptive words and phrases.

Example:

The young telephone operator quickly answered his ringing switchboard.

1.

2.

3.

4.

5.

2. The Compound Sentence   In the most basic terms, a compound sentence consists of two or more simple sentences joined by a *coordinating conjunction.* The three most commonly used coordinating conjunctions are "and," "but," and "or."

1. Picasso painted *Guernica,* <u>and</u> Van Gogh painted *Starry Night.*
2. Picasso painted *Guernica,* <u>but</u> he did not paint *Starry Night.*
3. Picasso must have painted *Guernica,* <u>or</u> the text-book would not have said he did.

EXERCISE 4

In the left-hand column, copy down the five most basic simple sentences you constructed in the first part of Exercise 1. Make each simple sentence a compound sentence by adding a coordinating conjunction in the center column and writing an appropriate simple sentence in the right-hand column.

Example:

Flem Snopes scratched	but	he could not stop the itch.

Simple Sentence from First Part of Exercise 1	Coordinating Conjunction	Additional Simple Sentence

New
Compound
Sentence

1.		

New
Compound
Sentence

2.		

New
Compound
Sentence

3.		

New
Compound
Sentence

4.		

New
Compound
Sentence

5.		

3. The Complex Sentence A simple sentence can also be called an *independent clause*. (A clause, like a sentence, has a subject and a predicate.) This name is more accurate because it gives an important fact about the simple sentence: that it is grammatically complete and can stand by itself. But if you add certain words to an independent clause, it cannot stand by itself, and is called a *dependent clause*.

Independent: Mark Twain wrote.
Dependent: <u>When</u> Mark Twain wrote . . .

Some of the most common dependency words are: after, although, because, before, if, since, that, though, unless, until, what, when, where, which, while, who, whom, and why.

When you add a dependent clause to an independent clause, you create a complex sentence. Notice how the dependent clause *depends* on the independent clause to complete the thought:

<u>When</u> Mark Twain wrote [he was extremely popular].

Here is another example:

Simple sentence
(Independent clause):   China is a republic.
Dependent clause: <u>Because</u> China is a republic . . .
Complex sentence: <u>Because</u> China is a republic, [it is no longer governed by an emperor].

EXERCISE 5   In the middle column below, copy down the five sentences you constructed in the second part of Exercise 1. In the left-hand column, write down a dependency word from the list above. In the right-hand column, write an appropriate simple sentence. You will now have a series of five complex sentences.

Example:

| While | cruel Flem Snopes furiously scratched | his mother ran for the flea powder. |

	Dependency Word	Sentence from Exercise 2	Simple Sentence
New Complex Sentence	1.		
New Complex Sentence	2.		
New Complex Sentence	3.		
New Complex Sentence	4.		
New Complex Sentence	5.		

4. The Compound-Complex Sentence   There is another type of sentence that is a hybrid of the compound and complex sentence. It most often consists of three basic parts: two independent clauses and a dependent clause.

Example:

independent clause   *independent clause*
[The world was young] and [the earth was not yet
dependent clause
cool], [when the rains began to fall].

When you join at least two independent clauses with at least one dependent clause you have a *compound-complex sentence:*

[While some students staged a protest against the proposed tuition increase], [others watched quietly] and [still others went about their daily business of attending classes].

EXERCISE 6

The following pairs of simple sentences are grammatically correct. In order to practice the skills you have just learned, change each pair into one *compound* sentence by adding a coordinating conjunction, and then into one complex sentence by adding a dependency word.

Example:

Simple: The cost of living is rising.
Many people are having a hard time paying their bills.
Compound: The cost of living is rising, and many people are having a hard time paying their bills.
Complex: Because the cost of living is rising, many people are having a hard time paying their bills.

1. Unemployment is increasing.
The welfare rolls are swelling.

2. A government job program will not work miracles.
   It could provide temporary employment for thousands.

3. Finding jobs for the unemployed is an important priority.
   Job training programs are equally important.

4. The cost of purchasing most goods and services is increasing.
   Even middle-class families are finding it difficult to obtain basic necessities.

5. The economy may improve.
   More people may be able to find work.

6. Members of minority groups are often the last hired.
   They are often the first fired when a company is forced to lay off workers.

7. Unemployment is high among skilled workers.
   It is much higher among unskilled workers.

8. Many college-educated people are finding themselves out of work.
   More high school–educated people are out of work.

9. In the late 1960s, there were too many engineers.
   In the 1970s, engineers are in demand.

10. Job prospects in the allied health professions look promising.
    Job prospects for teachers look bleak.

Using Sentence Patterns

When you write, you will find that each of the sentence patterns we have discussed is an option that you can use. Simple, compound, and complex sentences offer you a surprising range of subtlety and expression. But before you begin to use these patterns, you should have some idea of their strengths and weaknesses. Like paragraph strategies, sentence options should not be used arbitrarily. Your audience and purpose determine, to a large extent, which pattern to use and how effective it will be.

Short simple sentences can add a lot to your writing —when well handled. But they *can* be a problem. Too many simple sentences can make your writing sound like a first-grade primer. Used in appropriate situations (in personal writing, for instance), simple sentences can isolate ideas and can be used for emphasis. They can add directness and sincerity and can give the impression of excitement. Here is an example from a student paper on surfing:

> I caught the wave! I shifted my weight and dipped the nose of my board. In a fraction of a second I had slipped off the crest and was shooting through the curl. The foam curved around me and the wind pressed against my body. I was in ecstasy. Then my trouble started. In my excitement I lost concentration and my board tipped. I tried desperately to right it. It was too late. I flew through the air. I fought for breath in the twisting and churning surf. The next thing I remember was coughing and choking on the beach. My broken board was next to me and so was the lifeguard who had pulled me from the water.

The student writer used short, simple sentences to recreate the panic and breathless action she felt when she "wiped out" while surfing. Sentences like "I flew through the air. I fought for breath. . . ." effectively tell us what the experience was like.

Compound sentences, like simple sentences, are effective in personal and narrative essays. By linking independent clauses with coordinating conjunctions, compound sentences mirror the way we think when we talk: "I did this . . . and I did that." For this reason they can recreate conversations or give a conversational tone to your writing. Ernest Hemingway uses compound sentences effectively in his descriptive passages. These sentences from *The Sun Also Rises* are characteristic:

> We came down out of the mountains and through an oak forest, and there were white cattle grazing in the forest. Down below there were grassy plains and clear streams, and then we crossed a stream and went through a gloomy little village and started to climb again.

Compound sentences can also be used when you want to give two ideas equal weight. Coordinating conjunctions connect statements, examples, or facts without indicating any special relationship between them. For this reason, though, a string of compound sentences in an essay can make your writing sound monotonous and immature. Especially in academic writing, compound sentences should be used with care. Notice the effect they have in this student paragraph discussing research.

> I decided to do my research and I went to the library. I looked in the *Humanities Index* and I searched through the *PMLA Bibliography. Humanities Index* gave me five articles on William Carlos Williams, and *PMLA* gave me seven articles, one of which included a reference to Louis Zukofsky. Our library did not have the *William Carlos Williams Newsletter*, but I went to the University of Alabama's library and found it.

This paragraph conveys several ideas without providing the signals you need to relate them to one another. For instance, did the student look through *Humanities*

Index before *PMLA Bibliography?* Did the student go to University of Alabama's library because his university's library did not have the journal needed?

Complex sentences enable you to show how ideas stand in relation to each other. By placing important ideas in the independent clause you emphasize and display them clearly and unambiguously. Look at this rewritten version of the above paragraph, and notice how dependency words establish the relationship between ideas in each complex sentence:

> When I decided to do my research, I went to the library. After first looking in the *Humanities Index*, I searched through the *PMLA Bibliography*. *Humanities Index* gave me five articles and *PMLA* gave me seven, one of which included a reference to Louis Zukofsky. Because our library did not have the *William Carlos Williams Newsletter*, I went to the University of Alabama's library and found it.

Because of their subtlety and flexibility, complex sentences are used often in academic writing. With them you can show cause-and-effect relationships as well as time sequences and conditionality.

Cause and Effect: Because of the defective coupling, the gas tank ruptured on impact.

Cause and Effect: Since you are the most qualified in this area, you should go to the meeting in Denver.

Time Sequence: Until the residue in the bottom of the flask becomes clear, keep heating with a low flame.

Time Sequence: After Lillie Langtry had an affair with the prince, her social standing improved.

Conditionality: If Napoleon had not misjudged his strength, the outcome of the Battle of Waterloo might have been different.

Conditionality: Whether or not the meeting continues as scheduled, the participants must remain in the room.

These examples do not indicate the full range of conditions complex sentences can express, but they should give you some help in making decisions about when and how to make appropriate choices.

EXERCISE 7   Look back at the sentences you wrote in Exercise 6. Consider the simple, compound, and complex sentence options side by side. In each case, what are the advantages and disadvantages of each pattern?

CHAPTER 10

Sentence Style

Style is something that is a part of all our lives. It defines everything we do. But style, like everything else we do as human beings, is not fixed. We vary our styles as situations demand. For funerals we are solemn and restrained, and for picnics we are casual and relaxed. We do the same thing in our writing. We make our term papers and reports sound "academic" and formal, while our letters and journals sound loose and informal.

Writing style involves more than knowing when to use formal expressions or slang. Constructing sentences is part of it too, and so is word choice. As you already know, there are countless ways to express an idea, but some ways are more effective than others. For this reason, there is really no way to separate the content of a sentence from its style.

Sentence Economy

Meaningless words or phrases and needless repetition can make your sentences difficult to understand, or at least make your readers work too hard to extract your meaning.

1. Deadwood Words and phrases that do not add anything to the meaning of your sentences are called deadwood. They can be cut out without any loss of meaning. Many times they actually get in the way of clear communication.

Conversational expressions that find their way into your writing should be deleted.

Well, as I said before, there were several reasons for the popularity of communes in the late 1960s.

The entire first part of this sentence creates an informal atmosphere, and if that is not what you want, those five words should be dropped.

There were several reasons for the popularity of communes in the late 1960s.

Set phrases that are included for decoration should be eliminated, because they only pad a sentence and give it a false appearance of balance. Many students routinely begin their writing like this:

With reference to the question of psychological realism, Richardson can be said to create much more complex characters than Fielding.

This sentence should be revised to omit the long set phrase at its beginning, keeping the only important word, "psychological":

Richardson's characters are more psychologically complex than Fielding's.

Watch out for introductory phrases like "it is interesting to observe," "with respect to," "in regard to," "the fact that," and "as far as." They are often deadwood themselves, and sometimes they introduce whole sentences of padding.

"There is" and "there are" can often be eliminated without loss of meaning. Compare:

There are many people who live in my neighborhood who must work two jobs to make ends meet.

Many people who live in my neighborhood must work two jobs to make ends meet.

2. Redundancy   Needlessly saying the same thing twice

in the same sentence not only is clumsy writing but gets in the way of effective communication.

> In this modern world of today, a series of complex and complicated issues faces each and every citizen.

As you may have noticed, this sentence contains a number of redundancies. You should tighten it up by getting rid of the useless words and leaving only those that are needed to get the message across.

> Today we are faced with many complicated issues.

Each of the following sentences contains redundancies that could (and therefore should) be eliminated:

> In my opinion, I think this course was worthwhile.
> The teacher was very thorough in his teaching.
> The problems we discussed were basic and necessary to our subject.

Another kind of redundancy happens when you unnecessarily repeat the same words in a sentence.

> Many people in undeveloped nations have three enemies: one enemy is hunger, another is disease, and a third enemy is illiteracy.

This sentence should be rewritten to read:

> Many people in undeveloped nations have three enemies: hunger, disease, and illiteracy.

Or you may unnecessarily repeat the same words from sentence to sentence. You can remove this redundancy by combining the sentences into one.

> My mother considers herself a liberated woman because she has a job. Because she has a job she has financial independence.

Possible revisions:

> Because my mother's job has given her financial independence, she considers herself a liberated woman.
>
> or
>
> My mother considers herself a liberated woman because her job has given her financial independence.

CAUTION:

Repetition is not always redundant. Some is needed for clarity, emphasis, or other effects. The familiar children's tale of "The Three Little Pigs" would not be improved by revision.

Effective: "Little Pig! Little Pig! Let me come in. Open your door or I'll huff and I'll puff and I'll blow your house in!"

Ineffective: "Open your door or I will blow your house in!"

Notice how repetition in the following sentence emphasizes the writer's feelings toward his subject.

Effective: In the war-torn village there were too many troops, too many guns, and too many shattered lives.

Ineffective: In the war-torn village there were too many troops, guns, and shattered lives.

EXERCISE 1

Revise the following sentences to eliminate redundancies and meaningless words or expressions.

1. It is extremely interesting to observe that Einstein formulated the theory of relativity in 1905.
2. Durkheim believed that because of the fact that society was disintegrating, the suicide rate could be expected to rise.
3. Last summer my friend got a small bit part in a local production of *An Enemy of the People*.
4. Without a doubt, many of today's utopian theories

can be traced back to their original source in Rous-
seau's philosophy.

5. Due to the fact that one of the nuns was carrying
   a wicker basket, Holden gave her his absolutely
   last ten dollars.
6. Throughout the early part of this century, a tre-
   mendously large number of immigrants came to this
   country.
7. The M-1 was not an extremely accurate or straight-
   shooting rifle.
8. Competition helped to expand broader and greater
   markets.
9. The overthrow of Tsar Nicholas was an extremely
   unique event in Russian history.
10. Martin Luther King's "Letter from Birmingham
    Jail" illustrates the dominant spirit of courage and
    bravery that prevailed at the time it was written.

EXERCISE 2

Combine each of the following pairs of sentences into
one to eliminate redundancy.

1. Calvin Rendler works as a pipe fitter for the government. Working for the government, he is involved
   in many secret projects.
2. Reading science fiction is one of many college
   students' major interests. Science fiction provides
   many college students with hours of wonder and
   excitement.
3. Engelbert read an article in *Psychology Today*. In
   this article it said that people's names can influence
   their personalities.
4. One of Vermont's major industries is skiing. Because skiing is so popular there, many services exist
   solely for the benefit of skiers.
5. The state university is a co-op institution. Since it is
   a co-op, it has a five-year program.

EXERCISE 3

Combine each group of sentences into one sentence.
You may delete words to eliminate redundancy, and
you may add words or change verb forms where nec-

essary. Consider several possible combinations before deciding on one. Be prepared to discuss why you chose the one you did. When you have finished, double-check to make sure you have not written **any run-ons or sentence fragments.**

1. Somerset is the city.
2. The city has a mayor.
3. The mayor's name is L. F. Lansky.
4. L. F. Lansky stopped the schools from closing.

5. The mayor made a speech.
6. The speech was about the schools.
7. The schools needed money.

8. The people were angry.
9. The anger was about taxes.
10. Taxes were high.

11. The people voted.
12. The vote was on a bond issue.
13. The people showed their anger.
14. The people rejected the bond issue.

15. The schools had no money.
16. The schools would have to close.

17. Teachers would not teach.
18. Children would not learn.

19. The banks came to the rescue.
20. The banks lent money.
21. The money was for the schools.
22. The money was 50 million dollars.

23. The banks warned the schools.
24. The schools must cut waste.
25. The schools must balance their budget.
26. The schools must reduce teacher salaries.

27. Frank Brown headed the union.
28. Frank Brown was furious.
29. Frank Brown led a protest.

30. Teachers marched.
31. The march was in front of City Hall.
32. Teachers held signs.

33. The signs carried messages.
34. The messages protested pay cuts.

35. The mayor called a meeting.
36. The meeting was with Frank Brown.
37. The meeting was about the pay cuts.

38. The mayor reached an agreement.
39. The agreement was with Frank Brown.

40. The teachers returned.
41. The return was to work.
42. The children returned.
43. The return was to school.

44. The mayor made a speech.
45. The speech was on TV.
46. The mayor thanked Frank Brown.
47. The mayor thanked the teachers.
48. The thanks was for their cooperation.

Sentence Variety

1. What Is Sentence Variety? If you have ever listened to a speaker who drones on and on without ever changing his tone, you know how dull sameness can be. Good writers, like effective speakers, know how to vary the style of their presentation so their audiences do not get lulled into boredom. One way of making your essays more interesting is to vary the patterns of the sentences you write.

You already know one way to vary your sentence structure. By combining a series of short, simple sentences into compound and complex sentences, you can eliminate the choppiness of a paragraph like this:

> I always liked sports. At seven I got my first baseball glove. I practiced every day. Soon I was ready to try out for the local Little League. I was very small for my age. The team laughed when I went up to the plate with my bat. They soon stopped. I hit the ball over the left-field fence.

With a little bit of editing, this paragraph becomes:

> I always liked sports. When I was seven, my father bought me my first baseball glove. I practiced every day, and soon I was ready to try out for our local Little League. Because I was small for my age, the team laughed when I went up to the plate with my bat. They stopped, however, when I hit the ball over the left-field fence.

Experimenting with word order will help you to avoid beginning all your sentences in the same way. In the following example, every sentence begins with the subject or a pronoun referring to it.

> Ernest Hemingway wrote many books. His most famous is *The Sun Also Rises*. It is about a group of expatriates who live in Paris during the twenties. It portrays the meaningless lives they live as they move from one café to another. Jake Barnes is the major character. He typifies the sterility of this culture. He was wounded in the war and is sexually impotent. He is the Hemingway hero who most reflects the condition of modern man.

If you change the sentences so they do not all begin with "he" and "it," you get:

> The most famous of Ernest Hemingway's many books is *The Sun Also Rises*. Set in Paris during the twenties, it is about a group of expatriates who lead meaningless lives as they move from one café to another. Jake Barnes, the main character, typifies the sterility of this culture. He is sexually impotent as a result of a war wound and is the Hemingway hero who most reflects the condition of modern man.

Instead of making statements all of the time, try adding an occasional question, exclamation, or command, as the writer of the following paragraph does.

Why is it after thousands of auto deaths each year, countless motorists still do not use their seat belts? Investigators for the federal Department of Transportation have tried to answer the question. "I feel trapped when I wear them!" says one New Jersey driver. "It makes me nervous. What if the car caught fire and I couldn't get it off?" says a Wyoming woman. In an effort to eliminate these common complaints, the government has begun experimenting with a passive restraint system called the air bag.

Try varying the length of your sentences. Notice how this writer uses long and short sentences to vary the "landscape" of his paragraph.

Years passed before I saw my old house again. I was in town on a business trip when I decided to drive over and look at it. It was horrible. The large, gleaming white house I remembered from my youth was now old and run down. The paint was peeling. The front steps were rotted. The flower gardens my mother had planted around the yard had been replaced by a dense growth of ragged weeds. Nearly crying, I put my car into gear and drove away.

You can break down loose, sprawling compound sentences into more effective simple or complex sentences.

The way the governess in *The Turn of the Screw* attempted to solve her problems was not the best way, but she was young and wasn't worldly, and she did manage to solve her problems in the end, and rid the children of the ghosts without the help of her employer.

With some editing, this becomes:

The way the governess in *The Turn of the Screw* attempted to solve her problems was not the best way. Still, despite the fact that she was young and wasn't worldly, she did manage to solve her problems in the end, by ridding the children of the ghosts without the help of her employer.

2. Revising to Achieve Sentence Variety Each of the following paragraphs from different student essays is a series of logical, grammatical sentences. But because sentence patterns are so often repeated, the style is dull and wooden.

From "The Roots of Math Anxiety"

(1) Math anxiety can cause serious problems for students. (2) There is growing concern about it in high schools and colleges. (3) There is a feeling that it severely handicaps students. (4) It seems to affect more girls than boys. (5) It causes girls to stop taking math courses sooner than boys stop. (6) This can have a serious effect on their futures. (7) It can cause girls to avoid math-related careers. (8) There is no biological reason why females should not do well in math. (9) There may be social causes for math anxiety. (10) It may result from the conditioning girls receive as children and adolescents.

There is a good deal of information here, but the style is choppy—the paragraph reads like a list. All the sentences are simple sentences; almost all begin with "it" or "there," and there are very few transitional devices to link them together. All the sentences are declarative, and even though they vary somewhat in length, the variation shows little skill or apparent intent. By combining some of these sentences and eliminating deadwood and redundancy, you can achieve better variety.

Compare:

(1) There is a growing concern in high schools and colleges about math anxiety, which can cause serious problems for students. (2) Educators feel

that it severely handicaps students. (3) Math anxiety seems to affect more girls than boys, causing the girls to stop taking math courses sooner than their male counterparts. (4) This can have a serious effect on their futures in that girls may avoid math-related careers. (5) While there is no biological reasons why females should not do well in math, there may be social causes for math anxiety, possibly because of the conditioning girls receive as children and adolescents.

All but one of the "it" and "there" beginnings are gone. Also, the sentence patterns have been varied, since many of the simple sentences have been combined. The same information is supplied, but the revised paragraph has only five sentences instead of ten. The "list" is now a logically connected group of sentences.

Now look at the following paragraph:

From "The Hatfields and the McCoys"

(1) The Hatfields and the McCoys were two families. (2) They lived in the West Virginia and Kentucky mountains. (3) They began to feud right after the Civil War. (4) They were on different sides in the Civil War. (5) The Hatfields supported the South and the McCoys the North. (6) They had arguments over the Tug Fork, the river separating Kentucky and West Virginia. (7) In one of these conflicts a McCoy was killed. (8) They both encouraged their children to continue the hostilities. (9) Their feud grew even stronger because of a romance between a Hatfield boy and a McCoy girl. (10) They had a major brawl in 1882 and several McCoys were killed. (11) Their feud ended after a Hatfield was hanged for murder in 1890.

This could be an interesting paragraph, but as it reads now, it is another "list" of sentences, almost all of which begin with "they" or "their." The writer does have a lively subject and good detail, and he mixes simple, compound, and complex sentences, but by beginning every sentence with a pronoun referring back to his subject, he makes this a difficult paragraph to get through.

A possible revision:

(1) The Hatfields and the McCoys were two families who lived in the West Virginia and Kentucky mountains. (2) After the Civil War, in which the Hatfields supported the South and the McCoys the North, the two families began to feud. (3) In one of their many conflicts over the Tug Fork, the river separating Kentucky and West Virginia, a McCoy was killed. (4) Both families encouraged their children to continue the hostilities, which grew even stronger because of a romance between a Hatfield boy and a McCoy girl. (5) In 1882, several McCoys were killed in a major brawl, and the feud ended after a Hatfield was hanged for murder in 1890.

What changes have been made? Consulting the discussion of sentence variety, comment on this revision.

EXERCISE 4   This paragraph, taken from a review of a Bette Midler concert, varies the sentence structure to stimulate the reader's interest. Read it, and discuss what the student writer has done to achieve fluidity and variety in his sentences.

Bette Midler is one of the most versatile, beautiful young talents on the music scene today. Bette does not have a large following. Instead, she prefers to keep her act as personal as possible to satisfy her audience all she can. This means little commercialization and presentations to small audiences. Ms. Midler incorporates the audience into her show by inviting people onto the stage to sing, dance, and participate in skits. Bette Midler's biting sarcasm, wit, and knack for making the truth funny are well known to her fans and especially to her critics. Not only is Bette funny, talented, and beautiful, she is also kind, loyal, and generous to her friends. Looking past her good traits, though, it can be clearly seen that Bette is not a Girl Scout.

EXERCISE 5

Rewrite the following paragraphs, varying the sentence structure.

From "A Death in My Family"

Six months ago we had a tragedy in our family. It was a Tuesday afternoon. We received the news of my father's death. It was at this point in my life that I truly experienced the anxiety of losing somone close to me. This was a loss of a dominant part of my life. It made a lot of changes in my life. This tragedy was an experience I'll never forget.

From a book review of *Future Shock*

The implied purpose of the book *Future Shock* is to help us cope with the accelerated thrust of personal and social change. The book shows us what the future will develop into if the trend toward super-industrialism persists. The book was written to present the reader with a method by which to understand the changing future. The book makes the readers become "future conscious" and briefs them on the rapid change the future is leaning toward. Everyone, no matter how young or old, will be affected by the fast-changing pace of society.

11

Incorrect
Sentence
Patterns

Writing clear, complete sentences requires a lot of careful practice. Good writers know how to use the four major sentence patterns; they also know what can happen when incorrect patterns are used. These cause problems not only because they break grammatical rules, but also because they raise barriers to clear communication, barriers that prevent your readers from understanding exactly what you mean. It is up to you, as a writer, to recognize these incorrect sentence patterns and to correct them whenever they occur in your own essays.

The Sentence Fragment

A sentence fragment is a part of a sentence that is punctuated as if it were a complete sentence. Often these fragments sneak into your writing and act as confusing breaks to the smooth flow of your sentences. When you find a fragment in your writing, it will be one of the following types and should be corrected.

1. The statement that results when a dependent clause is punctuated as though it were a complete sentence is a fragment. (See the discussion of the complex sentence, pages 158–59.)

Simple sentence:	Hydrogen is an element.
Sentence fragment:	Because hydrogen is an element.
Compound sentence:	Hydrogen is an element, and water is a compound.
Sentence fragment:	While hydrogen is an element and oxygen is an element.

These fragments may be corrected in two ways: by eliminating the dependency word so that a simple or compound sentence remains, or by adding an independent clause to make a complex sentence.

Possible corrections:

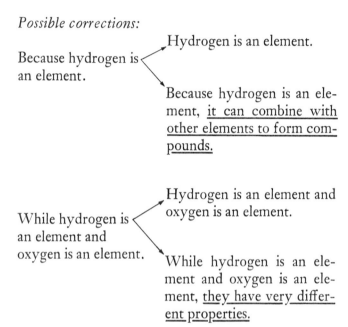

Because hydrogen is an element.

→ Hydrogen is an element.

→ Because hydrogen is an element, <u>it can combine with other elements to form compounds.</u>

While hydrogen is an element and oxygen is an element.

→ Hydrogen is an element and oxygen is an element.

→ While hydrogen is an element and oxygen is an element, <u>they have very different properties.</u>

EXERCISE 1

Each of these sentence fragments can be corrected in two ways. Rewrite each sentence without a dependency word. Then write a new complex sentence by combining the original fragment with a new independent clause.

1. If you can't stand the heat.
2. Although women did not get the vote until 1920.
3. Whether or not their intentions were honorable.
4. Before she became too interested in yoga.
5. Unless prison conditions can be improved immediately.
6. Even though stickball is hardly a national sport.
7. Since Marco Polo was only passing through.

8. Because he didn't wear a topcoat to his inauguration.
9. When insulin was discovered.
10. Before she purchased a ten-speed bike.
11. While he waited for the chicken to defrost.
12. Who all supported her decision to re-enter college.

2. A group of words that is missing a subject or predicate, or both, is also a sentence fragment.

Incorrect:	Some outstanding seventeenth-century scientists.
Possible corrections:	<u>Kepler</u>, <u>Galileo</u>, and <u>Newton</u> were some outstanding seventeenth-century scientists.
	or
	Some outstanding seventeenth-century scientists <u>challenged accepted theories.</u>
Incorrect:	Growing out of a search for realism in art.
Possible corrections:	Growing out of a search for realism in art, <u>impressionism nevertheless anticipated modern abstract art.</u>
	or
	<u>Most art historians consider that impressionism grew</u> out of a search for realism in art.
Incorrect:	To work in the mines for fifty years.
Possible corrections:	<u>Some miners expect</u> to work in the mines for fifty years.
	or
	To work in the mines for fifty years a <u>person must remain strong.</u>

Correct the following sentences by adding a phrase that supplies the missing subject and/or predicate.
1. Too many adjectives in one sentence.
2. The way he looked when he first caught sight of the Loch Ness monster.
3. To be more than just a rose on her husband's lapel.
4. The Mounties, searching the place where Sergeant Preston had last been seen.
5. A king with the power to rule the world.
6. Thinking it would be midnight at any moment.
7. Woody Guthrie, trying to make up his mind to leave Texas and head for California.
8. The kind of hamster with a lot of annoying little habits.
9. To know which way the wind is blowing.
10. A long way from Pittsburgh.

Run-on Sentences

A sentence fragment is less than a sentence; a run-on sentence is more. A run-on consists of two or more grammatically complete sentences carelessly stuck together without proper punctuation. There are two kinds of run-on sentences: *fused sentences*, in which two sentences are run together without any punctuation, and *comma splices*, in which two sentences are linked with only a comma.

1. Two simple sentences may be run together:

Fused sentence: [Lacrosse is a popular sport today] [it was invented by North American Indians].

Comma splice: [Lacrosse is a popular sport today], [it was invented by North American Indians].

2. A compound sentence can be run into a simple sentence:

Fused sentence: [She suspected asthma and she suspected chronic bronchitis] [she
wasn't sure about either diagnosis].

Comma splice: [She suspected asthma and she suspected chronic bronchitis], [she
wasn't sure about either diagnosis].

3. A complex sentence can also be incorrectly combined with a simple or compound sentence:

Fused sentence: [When gold was first discovered
in California, a westward migra-
tion began] [everyone dreamed of
getting rich].

Comma splice: [When gold was first discovered
in California, a westward migra-
tion began], [everyone dreamed of
getting rich].

Here are some ways to correct each of these three
errors:

1. Divide the run-on into separate sentences.

Lacrosse is a popular sport today. It was invented by
North American Indians.

She suspected asthma and she suspected chronic
bronchitis. She wasn't sure about either diagnosis.

When gold was first discovered in California, a
westward migration began. Everyone dreamed of
getting rich.

2. You could also use a semicolon instead of a period,
if the sentences are closely related.

Lacrosse is a popular sport today; it was invented
by North American Indians.

She suspected asthma and she suspected chronic
bronchitis; she wasn't sure about either diagnosis.

When gold was first discovered in California, a westward migration began; everyone dreamed of getting rich.

3. You could also correct a run-on sentence by adding a coordinating conjunction (and, but, or) between the clauses.

Lacrosse is a popular sport today, <u>and</u> it was invented by North American Indians.

She suspected asthma and she suspected chronic bronchitis, <u>but</u> she wasn't sure about either diagnosis.

When gold was first discovered in California, westward migration began, <u>and</u> everyone dreamed of getting rich.

Words like "however," "also," "therefore," and "thus" are *not* coordinating conjunctions and *cannot* be used to correct a run-on.

Incorrect

Fused sentence: She suspected asthma and she suspected chronic bronchitis however she wasn't sure about either diagnosis.

Comma splice: She suspected asthma and she suspected chronic bronchitis, however she wasn't sure about either diagnosis.

Words like "however," "also," "therefore," and "thus" are called conjunctive adverbs. Use a semicolon before a conjunctive adverb when it comes between two independent clauses.

Correction: She suspected asthma and she suspected chronic bronchitis; however, she wasn't sure about either diagnosis.

---

4. In some cases you could add a dependency word and make one of the sentences a dependent clause.

Although she suspected asthma and she suspected chronic bronchitis, she wasn't sure about either diagnosis.

EXERCISE 3

Correct the following run-on sentences by: (1) bracketing each sentence to divide it into the sentence patterns of which it is made, and (2) correctly combining these patterns to form sentences. In each case use as many of the methods illustrated above as you can.

1. Victoria reigned for over sixty years, Edward VII reigned for less than ten years.

2. Esther directed the family's cultural activities, therefore she seldom got a chance to cook.

3. Right to work laws are generally favored by businesses, however union members do not support them.

4. Fairy tales bore her they have no humor, sex, or violence.

5. Frances Perkins was the first woman Secretary of Labor she was appointed by President Roosevelt.

6. Tex walked slowly around the ranch, this gave his Levi's time to dry.

7. Nora knew she had to get away from Torvald, she couldn't stand being treated like a child forever.

8. Although it was reported that Tilden received a majority of the popular vote, Hayes was elected president this made the Republicans happy but disappointed the Democrats.

9. Mimi cooked a big pot of chili, so what if it was Thanksgiving?

10. Leadbelly played a twelve-string guitar, Pete Seeger plays a banjo.

Some simple rules for comma and semicolon usage will help you punctuate your sentences.

A **comma** has four principal uses:

1. To separate two independent clauses joined by a coordinating conjunction ("and," "but," "or," "nor," "for," "so," and "yet").

Example: The retina's long and narrow receptors are called rods, and the thicker receptors are called cones.

2. To separate words, phrases, and clauses in a series.

Example: Winston Churchill, Franklin Roosevelt, and Joseph Stalin met at Yalta in 1945.

3. To set off relatively long introductory or concluding remarks.

Examples: Contrary to most people's impression, the Cold War began soon after World War II.

The same situation may also be found in nursing homes, unfortunately for their elderly patients.

4. To set off a parenthetical phrase (a group of words that could be placed in parentheses).

Example: Each normal human cell contains a fixed number of chromosomes, forty-six, which in turn contain genes.

The **semicolon** has two principal uses.

1. To link two independent clauses that are not joined by a coordinating conjunction or separated by a period.

Example: In 1776 Adam Smith published *The Wealth of Nations;* that same year, the steam engine was invented by James Watt.

2. To separate elements of a series when those elements already contain commas.

Example: Three very important early periods in our history were the Paleolithic Age, characterized by peoples who hunted and devised stone implements; the Neolithic Age, whose peoples began to farm and settled in walled villages; and the Bronze Age, noted for elaborate jewelry and pottery, well-established kingdoms and aristocracy, and a history of warfare.

Misplaced Words or Phrases

Each language has a set of patterns that helps to determine what order the words and phrases in a sentence should follow. Sometimes there is more than one way to arrange a group of words. An adverb will sometimes follow a verb:

In the late nineteenth century, the use of railroads to transport passengers and freight <u>increased significantly</u>.

At other times the adverb may come first:

In the late nineteenth century, the use of railroads to transport passengers and freight <u>significantly increased</u>.

Adjectives, however, usually precede the noun they modify:

<u>Forced busing</u> to achieve <u>racial integration</u> is an extremely <u>controversial tactic</u>.

When word order rules are violated, the result is usually a sentence which is awkward and unclear.

<u>Busing forced</u> to achieve <u>integration racial</u> is an extremely <u>tactic controversial</u>

One way in which you can see how important word order is in a sentence is to compare these two sentences:

1. Validity and degree judged by standardization psychological be their objectivity of tests may reliability.
2. The glirby rep is lekking on the burblish ork.

The first sentence uses English words; the second, while composed primarily of nonsense words, uses English word order. While you do not know most of the words in sentence 2, the familiar word order, and helpful words like "the," "on," and "is," make you feel you *nearly* understand it. The first sentence, however, is anything but meaningful. What subject is under discussion? What is being judged? What are the criteria?

While no one who is a native speaker of English would say anything like sentence 1 by mistake, many of us make other errors that are almost as confusing. Misplaced words, especially modifiers, can give your readers a very hard time.

1. Misplaced Modifier In English, an adjective or adverb modifies (describes) a word by appearing *next* to it in a sentence. If you separate the modifying word or phrase from the word or phrase it modifies, some confusing and sometimes funny unintended meanings can result. Because a misplaced modifier can jumble your meaning, it can call your information into question, especially if it occurs in a final exam or a term paper. Consider the effect the following sentence would have on an instructor:

> Radio and television stations reported the news that the hijackers had freed their prisoners all over the world.

Because the student who wrote this sentence separated the modifier "all over the world" from the word it is supposed to modify ("stations"), his sentence implies that the hijackers had freed prisoners all around the world. What he meant to say was:

> Radio and television stations all over the world reported that the hijackers had freed their prisoners.

Most of the "misplaced phrase" errors you may make can be spotted if you read your sentences carefully. Making sure your sentences say exactly what you want them to say is an important part of the proofreading phase of your work. The following sentences, like the one above, need to be rewritten to clarify their meanings.

1. Le Corbusier saw the clean lines of the house he designed in his mind.
2. The delegate changed his vote at the General Assembly which was very unwise.
3. Magic was the forerunner of alchemy in the Middle Ages.

In each of these sentences, the confusion results from separating two parts of the sentence that should be connected.

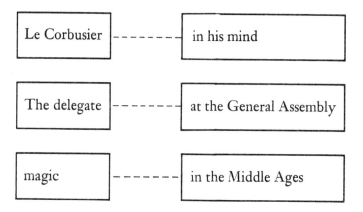

Rewritten, these sentences are much clearer.

1. In his mind, Le Corbusier saw the clean lines of the house he designed.
2. It was unwise for the delegate to change his vote at the General assembly.
3. In the Middle Ages, magic was the forerunner of alchemy.

EXERCISE 4

Correct these sentences by shifting a modifier in each, or, if necessary, by rewriting.

1. Your salesman told me that there was no provision for replacing the damaged merchandise in the contract.
2. Babo, a major character in *Benito Cereno*, attacked Captain Delano with a fierce grin.
3. Lowell saw canals on Mars through his telescope which surprised him.
4. Diane Arbus took pictures of subjects other photographers would not consider with her camera.
5. The detective reported that the vehicle hit a pothole he had been following.
6. Cyrano begged Roxanne to stay with him on his knees.
7. Ezra Pound wrote his long poem the *Cantos* with great difficulty.
8. We were dressed in blue and white gowns, our school colors.

9. If you do not return my security deposit I will be forced to take my case to a lawyer incurring a hardship.
10. I jumped from bed and watched the car rip through the large picture window in my underwear.

2. Dangling Modifier   Another "misplaced phrase" problem occurs when a part of the sentence is left hanging in air. This "dangling modifier" does not refer clearly to any other word or phrase in the sentence.

As crime fighters, this court decision seems very unfair.

Who are crime fighters? To whom does the court decision seem unfair? If you stopped reading after the first three words,

As crime fighters, . . .

and tried to guess the subject, you would probably continue the sentence:

As crime fighters, *the police* . . .

The actual subject, "this court decision," seems wrong. It *is* wrong. This is better:

As crime fighters, *the police* find this court decision very unfair.

EXERCISE 5   Revise the following sentences by making the subject clear. You may have to rewrite the sentence, or add a subject.

1. Living in Kansas City, the job would be convenient for me.
2. As a well-known poet, William Carlos Williams' *Paterson* will be read many years from now.

3. After adding 5 ml of hydrochloric acid, the flask should be heated until the liquid in it boils.
4. With approximately 30,000 students, time is still taken to be friendly at State University.
5. By limiting his study time to twenty minutes, failure seemed certain.
6. Being available around the house, many young children will try drinking just to see what it is like.
7. Coming from a small town in West Virginia, Houston was very difficult to get used to.
8. Not being able to play like other children, reading became increasingly important to the young Nathaniel Hawthorne.
9. Outflanked by Wellington's forces, the battle of Waterloo was decided and Napoleon surrendered.
10. By sprinkling iron filings around a magnet, the lines of the magnetic field are revealed.

Faulty Parallelism

Parallel lines run side by side and are alike in their direction. *Parallelism*, in any context, suggests similarity of angle and direction. When the parts of a sentence "match" grammatically, they are said to be parallel. When the elements of a sentence are not grammatically balanced, *faulty parallelism* results.

Correct: The hyperactive child is likely to misbehave frequently, <u>to have</u> a short attention span, and <u>to do</u> poorly in school.
Incorrect: The hyperactive child is likely <u>to misbehave</u> frequently, <u>to have</u> a short attention span, and <u>will do</u> poorly in school.

In the first sentence, all three of the things that characterize the hyperactive child are expressed as infinitive forms of verbs. In the second sentence, two verbs are infinitives and one is in the future tense. If you were given the first part of each sentence:

The hyperactive child is likely <u>to misbehave</u> frequently, <u>to have</u> a short attention span, and . . .

and asked to complete it, your first instinct would most likely be to add another verb of the same kind:

. . . and <u>to do</u> poorly in school.

Certain contexts, especially those that involve comparison or contrast, seem to call for parallel structures. A series of elements separated by commas within a sentence should be parallel.

Not: The mountains were tall, windswept, and the snow covered them.

But: The mountains were tall, windswept, and snow-covered.

The two halves of a compound sentence should usually be parallel.

Not: Kate Chopin wrote *The Awakening*, and "The Waking" is by Theodore Roethke.

But: Kate Chopin wrote *The Awakening*, and Theodore Roethke wrote "The Waking."

Or: *The Awakening* is by Kate Chopin, and "The Waking" is by Theodore Roethke.

Certain sets of words or phrases signal a series of related statements and call for parallel structure.

first   . . . second
not only . . . but also
both   . . . and
either   . . . or
neither   . . . nor

Not: The president <u>not only</u> vetoed [verb] the bill, <u>but also</u> he [pronoun] was against too much government spending.

But: The president <u>not only</u> vetoed [verb] the bill,
           <u>but also</u> said [verb] he was against too much
           government spending.

Notice that to achieve parallelism you may need to
match verbs, nouns, phrases, prepositions, or other
elements of your sentence.

Parallelism is important because it makes writing coherent and easy to follow. This is why it is used in situations where the writer wants to make sure the readers
interpret the information correctly. Exam questions
are often parallel in structure:

<u>Discuss</u> each character's emotional problems, <u>de-
scribe</u> his or her attempts to cope with them, and
<u>evaluate</u> the success of those attempts.

                              or

Discuss each character's emotional <u>problems,</u> his or
her <u>attempts</u> to cope with them, and the <u>success</u> of
those attempts.

Classified ads, which need to be clear, to the point,
and free of ambiguity, also use parallelism:

Wanted: College student with <u>desire</u> to learn sales
techniques, <u>interest</u> in cosmetics industry, <u>ability</u> to
make phone contacts, and <u>access</u> to car.

Because parallelism helps your reader to keep track
of your statements, you may want to use it on long
papers or on exams. (Look back to Sections I and II,
and notice how well-constructed topic sentences can
set up a parallel structure in an entire essay.) Another
situation that calls for parallelism is résumé writing,
where balance and rhythmic repetition can help emphasize your qualifications to a potential employer.

EXERCISE 6   Underline the parallel devices used in this excerpt from
                     a résumé, and explain why they are effective. You may

want to consider parts of speech, punctuation, coordination, and even content.

Sept. 1981–June 1982
Assistant Recreation Worker
Summit Presbyterian Church

Duties included: sharing responsibility for supervision of ten 6-year-olds, six 7-year-olds, and nine 8-year-olds in a parent-directed after-school program for first- to third-graders; purchasing equipment, snacks, and art supplies; attending parent/staff meetings; writing reports on each child's adjustment to the program; planning field trips, organizing sports and games, and designing arts and crafts projects; and writing a research paper analyzing the after-school program for a college course in recreation.

EXERCISE 7

The first two sentences below are part of an answer to an essay exam in a sociology course, No. 3 is taken from a bio lab report, and No. 4 is from a botany midterm. Underline the parallel elements in each of the sentences and explain what makes them parallel.

1. Personal power is the freedom to choose one's own destiny; social power is the ability to affect public affairs.
2. Authority is formal or official power based on the prerogatives that legitimately go with an office or position; influence is informal power based on know-how and "know-who."
3. The purpose of the inquiry was to find out how pepsin influences protein digestion, and how temperature affects enzyme activity.
4. The role of the perianth of a flower is to attract the insects to it by its bright color and by its distinctive odor.

EXERCISE 8

Now identify the parallel elements in a more complete answer to a question on that botany midterm. See if

you can explain—without any knowledge of botany—
why effective use of parallelism strengthens the answer.

Question: Discuss the composition and origin of the
tissue know as periderm.

Answer: Periderm tissue consists of the phellogen
(cork cambium), which is formed by the
cortex; phellem (or cork), which is produced by the phellogen and is formed on its
outer side; and phelloderm (or "cork skin"),
which is formed by the phellogen toward
its inner side.

EXERCISE 9   Each of the following sentences has elements that
should be parallel but are not. Rewrite them so they are
logical and easy to understand, and then underline the
parallel elements.

1. Psychologists are concerned with problems like
   finding the best treatment for alcoholism or drug
   addiction, designing surveys to measure public
   opinion, and how children can be taught to read.
2. His career depends upon kissing babies and also he
   makes speeches.
3. First he took out a large beaker, set up the other
   materials, and finally he began the experiment.
4. Joe Keller told his partner that he was sick with
   the flu and go ahead and send out the cracked
   cylinder heads.
5. *Some of My Best Friends* focuses on anti-Semitic
   incidents in fraternities, in housing, and on the part
   of private clubs.
6. Sugar is made up of carbon and hydrogen and
   also contains oxygen.
7. Adolescence is sandwiched between childhood and
   an adult.
8. A cockroach is between half an inch to two inches
   in length.

9. I find Bio lab unpleasant because I hate to draw and the smell of formaldehyde.
10. Two examples of the organization's "shady deals" were plans to create monopolies, and having companies charge the city higher prices than necessary for utilities.

Shifting Perspectives

Closely related to faulty parallelism is another kind of imbalance, created when you shift certain gears in the middle of a sentence (or, of course, a paragraph or essay). These abrupt shifts can cause confusion just as faulty parallelism or misplaced phrases can.

Here are some examples:

1. Shift from Past to Present Tense

Confusing: I <u>was</u> really enjoying the quiet when a stranger <u>sits</u> down next to me and <u>starts</u> whistling.

Clear: I <u>was</u> really enjoying the quiet when a stranger <u>sat</u> down next to me and <u>started</u> whistling.

2. Shift from Active to Passive Voice

Confusing: Arthur Miller <u>wrote</u> *The Crucible* to criticize "witch hunts" for Communist sympathizers, and it <u>was</u> also <u>written</u> to show how easily people are swayed by others' opinions.

Clear: Arthur Miller <u>wrote</u> *The Crucible* to criticize "witch hunts" for Communist sympathizers, and to show how easily people are swayed by others' opinions.

3. Shift from Singular to Plural

Confusing: <u>A person</u> should always be sure to keep <u>their</u> head in an emergency.

Clear: <u>A person</u> should always be sure to keep <u>his or her</u> head in an emergency.

or

<u>People</u> should always be sure to keep <u>their</u> heads in an emergency.

4. Shift from First Person to Third Person

Confusing: <u>We</u> love the city, but <u>one</u> is aware that changes are needed.

Clear: <u>We</u> love the city, but <u>we</u> are aware that changes are needed.

5. Shift from Statement to Question

Confusing: Dave, in Richard Wright's story "The Man Who Was Almost a Man," must decide <u>whether he should</u> stay a boy in the South or <u>should he</u> run away.

Clear: Dave, in Richard Wright's story "The Man Who Was Almost a Man," must decide <u>whether he should</u> stay a boy in the South or <u>whether he should</u> run away.

EXERCISE 10

Tense shifts tend to occur most often in narrative writing, when you are asked to write a piece of fiction, an autobiographical account, a précis or summary of someone else's ideas, or a plot summary. A student began an analysis of the central character in J. D. Salinger's *The Catcher in the Rye* like this:

> In *The Catcher in the Rye* Holden Caulfield found himself unable to cope with society. One of the main reasons why he could not cope is that he feels everyone and everything around him is phony. He also felt that no one would listen to him, and he has difficulty communicating with people. Because of this inability to communicate, he is alienated from everyone. Eventually, he left school and tries to live it up in New York for a few days. During this time, he was probably doing some soul searching.

Rewrite this paragraph to correct tense shifts that may be confusing. (Note: present tense is often easiest to handle when writing plot summaries.)

EXERCISE 11   Students in a first-year biology class were asked on a lab quiz to review the process of dissecting a shark, a procedure they had all been involved in for several weeks. While few students had much trouble remembering the details of the procedure, nearly all had a great deal of difficulty in communicating the step-by-step process. A survey of some of their answers showed that their main problem was maintaining consistent points of view—that is, avoiding confusing shifts. The following is one student's description:

Dissecting a shark is a very simple procedure. The first thing a student must do is to rinse the area which they are going to cut. Then prepare to make your first cut by taking a pencil and drawing a horizontal line across the anterior margin of each pectoral fin, and a horizontal line is then drawn across the posterior margin of each pelvic fin. Now knead the flesh of the belly so the skin can be easily pulled up without injuring the internal organs. After doing this preliminary work, the student should take their scissors from the dissecting kit. Keeping the rounded edge down so as not to cut any internal organs, cut along your pencil lines. The incision is made from the bottom of the pectoral fins to the top of the pelvic fins. Then the student should form an "I" incision by making two cross-sectional cuts anterior to the pectoral and pelvic fins. At this point, I was able to open up the flaps of the skin and muscle like a book. Now, wash the preservatives out of the shark. Then, you should displace as much of the digestive tract as possible. Cut off the three liver lobes, and now you should be able to see the heart. One can then cut each of the arteries that leads to the heart, cut away the muscle tissue that surrounds

the heart, and the heart may be extracted from the
body of the shark. As the dissection proceeded,
sketches were made of the various systems.

Rewrite this description to eliminate confusing shifts.

Agreement Errors

Agreement refers to the relationship between different
elements within a sentence. When two related elements,
subject and verb or pronoun and antecedent, show the
same number and person (and, in the case of pronouns,
gender) they are said to agree.

1. Subject-Verb Agreement A verb should agree in
number with its subject. Singular subjects should have
a singular verb, and plural subjects should have plural
verbs.

Singular: Advertising conveys a manufacturer's
message to the public.

Singular: Franz Liszt was Wagner's son-in-law.

Plural: Douglas MacArthur and George Patton
were generals during World War II.

Plural: Ezra Pound's *Pisan Cantos* and William
Carlos Williams's *Paterson* have influ-
enced poetry written since the 1950s.

Although the examples above are fairly straightforward, there are some special situations that might
cause you trouble. The best way for you to eliminate
subject-verb agreement problems from your writing is
to review the following constructions periodically.

a. Singular subjects connected by "and" are usually
plural and require a plural verb.

Alexander Pope and John Dryden were writers during the Neoclassic period.

Tempera paint and stirrers are contained in the package.

Sometimes, however, a compound subject can be considered as a unit and, thus, take a singular verb.

My friend and companion has left me. [one person]

Ham and eggs is a typical high-cholesterol breakfast.

"Each" or "every" before singular subjects usually means that each subject is considered individual and takes a singular verb.

Each officer and enlisted person was given a commendation.

Every man and woman was required to fill out this form.

b. Singular subjects preceded by "either . . ." or "neither . . ." usually take a singular verb.

Either a glass or a lead container is required.

Neither Hans Castorp nor his cousin knows for certain how long Mary will stay at the sanitarium.

c. Subjects such as "each," "either," "neither," "one," "everyone," "anyone," and "everyone" take singular verbs.

Everyone in the freshman class attends orientation.

Each is labeled and stored according to its size and density.

Neither requires much observation.

d. When two subjects, one singular and the other plural, are connected by "or," "nor," or "but," the verb agrees with the nearest subject.

> Neither the corporation <u>nor</u> its lawyers <u><u>were</u></u> found to have liability.

> Not only local primaries, <u>but</u> also the party convention <u><u>determines</u></u> who will be nominated for the presidency.

e. Nouns that look plural but are singular in meaning take a singular verb.

> <u>Physics <u>is</u></u> the study of matter and energy and their interactions.

> <u>States' rights <u>is</u></u> an important issue to consider when studying the Civil War.

Titles, even when in plural form, should be considered as a unit and given a singular verb.

> *Fields of Fire* by James Webb <u><u>captures</u></u> the fury of combat in Vietnam.

> The *<u>London Times</u> <u>is</u>* one of the world's most respected papers.

f. Don't be thrown by words or phrases that come between a subject and its verb.

> <u>Repeating</u> these maneuvers <u><u>enables</u></u> you to save a choking victim.

> Rising <u>interest rates</u> along with inflation <u><u>have</u></u> characterized our economy for the past three years.

EXERCISE 12   Some of the following sentences have subjects and verbs that do not agree. If a sentence is correct, underline the subject and the verb. If a sentence is incorrect, make the necessary changes, again underlining the subject and the verb.

1. William Blake's *Songs of Experience* is a group of poems that present an ironic view of childhood.
2. COBOL, BASIC, and FORTRAN are three commonly used computer languages.
3. The instructor, along with the class, has agreed to meet two hours on Wednesday.
4. Celine's Paris or Durrell's Alexandria are examples of fictionalized cities.
5. Neither Wisconsin nor Minnesota have a population equal to that of New York.
6. The planting of these shrubs are necessary to shade the house and reduce fuel consumption.
7. Engineering ethics is a course required of every sophomore engineering student.
8. A sample population or selected specimens are adequate for this study.
9. Surprisingly, newspapers considered Edward Everett, not Lincoln, the best orator at Gettysburg.
10. Ways and Means is one of the most influential congressional committees.

2. Pronoun-Antecedent Agreement Just as verbs must agree with their subjects, a pronoun must agree with its antecedent—the word or group of words to which it refers. A pronoun agrees with its antecedent if both show the same number. In other words, a singular antecedent should have a singular pronoun, and a plural antecedent should have a plural pronoun.

Singular: <u>Odysseus</u> never forgot <u>his</u> homeland.

Plural: <u>Botanists</u> devote <u>their</u> professional lives to the study of plants.

Traditionally, antecedents that did not specify gender were referred to by a masculine noun. Recently, however, the tendency has been to recognize the individuality of both men and women and to include both male and female pronouns.

> A <u>teacher</u> should try to make <u>his or her</u> objectives clear.

This construction works well in some cases, but in situations where there are a number of pronoun references it can be confusing or cumbersome. In these cases you can either apply the traditional rule or avoid the situation by making the antecedent plural.

> <u>Students</u> should hand in <u>their</u> assignments on time.

The following special situations can cause problems with pronoun-antecedent agreement.

a. Indefinite pronouns such as "each," "either," "neither," "one," "anyone," "everybody," "nobody," and "somebody" usually take a singular pronoun.

> <u>Each</u> culture can be judged by <u>its</u> treatment of the sick and the elderly.

> <u>Neither</u> woman reported side effects after <u>her</u> treatment.

> Soon after the death of a loved one, <u>anyone</u> can find <u>him- or herself</u> experiencing depression.

b. Two or more nouns connected by "and" usually take a plural antecedent; two or more singular antecedents connected by "or" or "nor" will take a singular pronoun.

Byron and Shelley were known for their passion for poetry and revolution.

Neither Germany nor Japan lost its industrial capacity after World War II.

Either Bergman or Fellini will have his films shown at the festival.

If one antecedent is singular and the other is plural and they are joined by "or" or "nor," the pronoun agrees with the antecedent nearest it.

Neither the brief nor the depositions had reached their destination by the deadline. [*Depositions* is closer to the pronoun *their*.]

Free ions or even an occasional CS_2 molecule will find its way into the tube. [CS_2 *molecule* is closer to the pronoun *its*.]

c. A collective noun takes either a singular or plural antecedent, depending on whether it is to be considered as a unit or as a number of individuals or things.

Singular: The jury carried out its duty and was discharged.

Singular: The crowd surged forward and raised its voice in one enormous growl.

Plural: The Senate voted to recess early in order to return to their campaigns.

Plural: The class of 1965 have gone their individual ways.

One final word of caution. A pronoun should point clearly to its antecedent. There should be no question in a reader's mind what the reference is. Vague and confusing references should be clarified when you revise.

Vague reference: Because he likes landscaping better than groundskeeping, he avoids it.

Revision: Because he prefers landscaping, he avoids groundskeeping.

Vague reference: The prisoner waited nervously as they decided his fate.

Revision: The prisoner waited nervously as the jury decided his fate.

EXERCISE 13   Choose the correct pronoun from within the parentheses.

1. A cold is usually caused by one of the many rhinoviruses. Once started (it, they) must run (its, their) course.
2. The City Council is able to vote (itself, themselves) raises.
3. Each of the franchisers contributes some of (his or her, their) profits to the parent company.
4. Neither accountant was satisfied with (his or her, their) performance during the internal audit.
5. The faculty could not decide what benefits (it, they) wanted in the new contract.
6. Neither the reactor vessel nor the pipes retained its, their) protective covering.
7. Indians and sometimes a freed slave spent (his or her, their) time in the settlement.
8. The class will vote for (its, their) officers this Thursday.
9. The World Court and the United Nations both have as (their, its) goal world peace.
10. Everybody has (his or her, their) own ideas about what to do about the oil shortage.

SECTION **IV**

THE
WORDS

Choosing the right words in your sentences will help you to communicate your ideas to your readers accurately and effectively. Often, however, choosing the right word depends on knowing how to detect the wrong word. You may need to change a word because you have already overused it in your essay, or because it turns out not to mean exactly what you thought it meant. Or a word may be wrong for the context in which you have placed it, perhaps too formal or informal for that context. A good sense of how to use words is a skill that every writer should develop.

CHAPTER 12

Choosing
the
Right Word, Part I

Overused Words

While revising an essay you have just completed, you may discover that you have repeated some key words or phrases over and over. Although repeating the ideas these words express may be necessary for your essay, reading the same word or phrase so often is boring. You have two basic options to avoid overusing key words: substituting a pronoun, or substituting a word or expression that means about the same thing. In the following paragraph from a student essay about the Philadelphia 76ers, for instance, the name of the team appears at least once in every sentence.

The Sixers have had various problems early in the season, but there is no need for any worrying by the Sixers fans. The Sixers are a relatively new inexperienced team, but with practice during the regular season, the Sixers will become one of the most awesome teams in basketball history. Sixers fans will then see that the players are worth their salaries and that the Sixers' general management made the correct decision in signing these key players for the team.

1. Substituting a Pronoun Here is a possible revision. The pronouns "they" and "their" are substituted for "the Sixers," with the following results:

The <u>Sixers</u> have had various problems early in the season, but there is no need for any worrying by <u>their</u> fans. <u>They</u> are a relatively new and inexperienced team, but with practice during the regular season, the <u>Sixers</u> will become one of the most awesome teams in basketball history. <u>Their</u> fans will then see that the players are worth their salaries and that the <u>Sixers'</u> general management made the correct decision in signing these key players for the team.

The word "Sixers" is now used three times rather than six, and, as a result, the entire paragraph seems smoother and less repetitious.

2. Substituting a Synonymous Word or Expression

You could also revise the same paragraph in a way that uses not only pronouns but also other words that mean about the same.

The <u>Philadelphia Seventy-Sixers</u> have had various problems early in the season, but there is no need for any worrying by <u>their</u> fans. The <u>team</u> is relatively new and inexperienced, but with practice during the regular season, <u>it</u> will become one of the most awesome in basketball history. <u>Sixers</u> fans will then see that the players are worth their salaries, and that the <u>club's</u> general management made the correct decision in signing these key players for the team.

In this revision, "Sixers" appears only once. The synonyms "club," "team," and "Philadelphia Seventy-Sixers" and the pronouns "their" and "it" provide variety.

EXERCISE 1   In the following paragraph, vary the choice of words by substituting different synonyms or pronouns for the words "sports," "increase(d)," "sales," and "equipment."

Sales of sports equipment have greatly increased in recent years. Sales of tennis rackets, bowling balls, ski equipment, and golf equipment are all prime examples of this increase. Tennis rackets probably best demonstrate the increased sports equipment sales because stores always seem to be running out of them. Manufacturers have also spent millions of dollars on the development of sports equipment that makes people seem to play better than they really can, such as specially weighted bowling balls.

Inexact Word Usage

At times you may find yourself using words you have invented yourself; these are called "coinages." All words were "coined"—that is, somebody made them up—at some time or other. And many words are still being coined to fill new needs, for example in the sciences, or to add vitality to speech, such as slang. But some coinages are mistakes, the result of guesses at a word the writer doesn't quite know. These invented words—words like "expellment" (expulsion), "prioritize" (set priorities), "orientate" (orient), or "inpolite" (impolite)—may confuse your readers. If you feel uneasy about a word you have used, check it in a dictionary.

When you revise, you may also find that you have used some of your words incorrectly. Often, because you are unsure of the exact meaning of a word, you can confuse one word or phrase with another.

1. Confusing Two Words Two words that sound alike can easily be mixed up. Common examples include substituting "lay" for "lie" and "set" for "sit," or confusing "conscious" and "conscience." (See "Commonly Confused Word Pairs" on pp. 207 ff. for a more complete list.) Another example is:

Many home smoke detectors emit a negligent amount of radioactivity.

In this sentence, the student confused "negligent" (careless) with "negligible" (minor; unimportant).

One part of speech can also be confused with another. Examples are "dominate" and "dominant," "image" and "imagine," or "paralysis" and "paralyze." Another example is:

My landlord asked me to <u>vacant</u> my apartment.

In this sentence, the student confused the adjective "vacant" (empty; unoccupied) with the verb "vacate" (leave the premises).

Sometimes, especially on exams when you may be tense or hurried, you may write things like "sacred <u>vowels</u>" when you mean "sacred <u>vows</u>," or "<u>prompt</u> and circumstance" when you mean "<u>pomp</u> and circumstance." You know what you meant to write, and you will catch these slips if you take the time to read your paper carefully before handing it in.

EXERCISE 2

Using a dictionary if necessary, define each of the words underlined below, and explain why it is used incorrectly. When you have done this, use each of the words correctly in a new sentence. Finally, rewrite the entire paragraph, supplying words that make sense in the context of the original paragraph.

Saul Bellow has a <u>repetition</u> for being a talented novelist, and he certainly deserves it. <u>Exceeding</u> not only in style but in characterization as well, Bellow is truly a fine writer. In fact, he was <u>rewarded</u> the Nobel Prize for his work. Of all Mr. Bellow's novels, I have the greatest <u>likeness</u> for *Herzog.* Moses Herzog is one of Bellow's most famous <u>caricatures.</u> It is true that many readers <u>foresee</u> him as a weak, neurotic person, and that Herzog's many problems may <u>subtract</u> from some readers' enjoyment of the novel. Perhaps, they feel, Bellow should try to create more <u>virulent</u> characters instead of victims. But I found Herzog to be a realistic, sympathetic person. I thought, however, that the novel was weak in another respect. I felt it contained more than an <u>efficient</u> number of pages. After all, too much <u>sediment</u> in a novel can be a cover for a weak plot.

1. Repetition	6. Foresee
2. Exceeding	7. Subtract
3. Rewarded	8. Virulent
4. Likeness	9. Efficient
5. Caricatures	10. Sediment

2. Commonly Confused Word Pairs The following glossary lists words that are commonly misused, misspelled, or confused:

accept, except *Accept* is a verb that means *to receive. Except* is a preposition meaning *with the exclusion of*.

I will <u>accept</u> delivery of this package.

All the children went into the next reading group <u>except</u> John, who had a perceptual dysfunction.

access, excess *Access* means *ability to enter or approach. Excess* means *more than usual*.

The Watergate burglars easily gained <u>access</u> to the office of the Democratic National Committee.

After making the initial incision, trim away the <u>excess</u> tissue.

affect, effect *Affect* is a verb meaning *to influence. Effect* is a noun meaning *result*.

The scarlet letter Hester wore not only <u>affected</u> her behavior, but also the way the townspeople reacted toward her.

The many wars during the fourteenth century had an <u>effect</u> on France's economy.

Effect as a verb means *to bring about.*

The city charter provides for a recall petition to <u>effect</u> a change in local government.

allusion, illusion   *Allusion* is a *reference. Illusion* is a *deceptive impression.*

In *The Magic Mountain* Thomas Mann makes an <u>allusion</u> to Goethe's *Faust.*

Only by ignoring the rapidly rising interest rates of recent months can one maintain the <u>illusion</u> of a healthy bond market.

among, between   *Among* refers to at least three persons or things. *Between* refers to two.

The flower's pistil, a red stalk, can be seen <u>among</u> a number of thin yellow stamens.

The information about the merger is secret and is to be kept <u>between</u> you and me.

amount, number   *Number* is used with countable items. *Amount* refers to a *total measurable in units.*

General Motors is producing small cars in a <u>number</u> unprecedented in its history.

The <u>amount</u> of pain a patient experiences can be minimized with medication.

beside, besides *Beside* is a preposition meaning *at the side of. Besides* means *in addition.*

The atomic reactor is located <u>beside</u> the small community of Middletown, Pennsylvania.

<u>Besides</u> the issue of the West Bank settlements, the Egyptian and Israeli negotiators discussed the future of Jerusalem.

can, may *Can* expresses *ability or power. May* suggests *permission or willingness.*

With new lightweight cements we <u>can</u> design buildings that would have been impossible to build ten years ago.

According to the new tax regulations, a homeowner <u>may</u> deduct fifteen percent of the cost of all energy-saving improvements from his or her tax bill.

continual, continuous *Continual* means *recurring at intervals or in rapid succession. Continous* means *uninterrupted.*

The <u>continual</u> wars that have plagued Vietnam have made economic development impossible.

<u>Continuous</u> overuse of the land by planting crops such as cotton and tobacco depleted the soil.

disinterested, uninterested *Disinterested* means *unbiased. Uninterested* means *apathetic or not interested.*

As a <u>disinterested</u> observer, I was able to resolve the dispute between them.

Because he was <u>uninterested</u> in modern art, he did not go to the Picasso exhibit.

emigrant, immigrant An *emigrant* is *someone who has left a country*. An *immigrant* is *someone who has arrived in a country*.

fewer, less *Fewer* is used when *counting things that can be numbered separately*. Less is used in *comparing amounts that can't be counted separtaely*.

There are <u>fewer</u> songs now that deal with social issues than there were in the 1960s.

The students in the other class have <u>less</u> work than we do.

formally, formerly *Formally* means *according to form. Formerly* means *previously*.

The demands of classic style <u>formally</u> dictate the size of the columns and the distance between each one.

The book had <u>formerly</u> been test-marketed under a different title.

imply, infer *Imply* means *to suggest. Infer* means *to draw a conclusion*.

The editorial <u>implied</u> that the mayor's actions were unethical, if not illegal.

From James Joyce's *The Dubliners* we can <u>infer</u> the social conditions that existed in a working-class neighborhood in Dublin at the turn of the century.

lie, lay *Lie* is an intransitive verb (one that does not take an object) meaning *to recline. Lay* is a transitive verb meaning *to place or set down*.

Present	Past	Perfect
lie	lay	lain
lay	laid	laid

loose, lose *Loose* is an adjective meaning *unrestrained. Lose* is a verb meaning *to misplace.*

Jefferson saw this country as a <u>loose</u> confederation of states bound together by a small central government.

It is possible to win the popular vote but still <u>lose</u> the election.

past, passed *Past* refers to something that has *already happened. Passed* is *the past action of passing.*

In the <u>past</u>, scientists thought the atom was an indivisible particle.

Even though the time limit specified in the treaty had <u>passed</u>, both sides acted as if the agreement were still in force.

persecute, prosecute *Persecute* means *to harass persistently. Prosecute* means *to seek legal action because of a crime.*

Throughout the reign of Elizabeth I of England, Catholics were periodically <u>persecuted</u>.

The city can <u>prosecute</u> violators of the health code only when a complaint is filed.

Precede, proceed *Precede* means *to go or come before. Proceed* means *to continue on.*

Copernicus <u>preceded</u> Galileo and anticipated many of his discoveries.

After their defeat, the Germans <u>proceeded</u> to withdraw from Russia during the winter.

prejudice, prejudiced *Prejudice* is a noun meaning *a preconceived judgment or opinion. Prejudiced* is the participle or adjective form.

<u>Prejudice</u> against a large number of ethnic groups, especially Jews, characterized Nazi politics during the early 1930s.

Because of the <u>prejudiced</u> remarks of the judge, the defendant was granted a new trial.

principal, principle As a noun, *principal* means *leader or head*. As an adjective it means *main*. *Principle* is a noun that means *theory or rule*.

The department heads are directly responsible to the <u>principal</u>, who, in turn, reports to the district superintendent.

He cited lack of funds as the <u>principal</u> reason for his decision to withdraw from the race.

One <u>principle</u> of chess is that you never leave your king unprotected.

raise, rise *Raise* is a transitive verb meaning *to lift up. Rise* is a verb meaning *to get or go up*.

Every morning we would get up at 6:00, quickly dress, and go outside to watch them <u>raise</u> the flag.

When the stock market <u>rises</u>, it is said to be bullish.

sit, set *Set* is a transitive verb that means *to put something down. Sit* means *to occupy a place by sitting*.

She <u>set</u> the pizza box on the table and went to get the wine.

When the national anthem was over, the fans were able to <u>sit</u> down again.

3. Blending Two Expressions Sometimes students confuse two expressions and accidentally "blend" them. The result is an incorrect phrase that jumbles together the two correct ones. For example:

TV is <u>setting a bad influence</u> on children.

It is perhaps true that TV <u>is a bad influence</u> on children. It can also <u>set a bad example</u> for them. But influences are not set.

EXERCISE 3

In each of the following underlined phrases, identify the two phrases the writer has confused. Then rewrite the paragraph substituting one of these phrases for each blend.

Scientists probably possess the <u>greatest desire</u> for success <u>than</u> anyone else. As soon as they <u>see a glimpse</u> of their future, they <u>persist to pester</u> their teachers for more and more information. Many begin their "careers" even before they begin school. Often, a chemistry set <u>cultivates them toward</u> a love of science. As they grow older, they begin to understand the importance of using the educational system <u>to its full advantage</u>, and feel that if they aren't learning from every experience, school isn't <u>doing its purpose.</u> It may be said that scientific achievement <u>falls under the generalization</u> of progress. The United States, for example, <u>accomplished a great deed</u> when it became the first country to send men to the moon, and Watson and Crick, two <u>world known</u> scientists, contributed to scientific progress by studying DNA. Observation of the methods of scientists has revealed their concern with complete accuracy, with minute detail, with precision: in some scientific measurement, even a discrepancy of <u>a half an inch</u> is too great. Despite the enormous challenges, difficulties, and responsibilities encountered in their professions, most scientists, when asked whether they have had second thoughts about their career choice, would probably answer with a <u>cool and collective</u> "no."

1. greatest desire . . . than

2. see a glimpse of

3. persist to pester

4. cultivates them toward

5. to its full advantage

6. doing its purpose

7. falls under the generalization

8. accomplished a great deed

9. world known

10. a half an inch

11. cool and collective

Idioms

An idiom is an accepted phrase that has a built-in meaning that is independent of the meanings of each of its words. Expressions like "to bring about," or "to put up with" do not make sense taken word for word, but "sound right" to anyone who speaks English. Idiomatic usage is largely determined by custom; people agree to use an idiom to mean a certain thing regardless of its literal meaning. If you have ever struggled to memorize Spanish or French idioms, or to figure them out when you don't know them, you know how illogical and confusing these expressions can be at first to a person learning the language. Both languages, for instance, ask not "What is your name?" but "How do you call yourself?" Even native speakers of Spanish or French—or English—sometimes have trouble using idiomatic expressions correctly.

EXERCISE 4   Which of the sentences below include acceptable idiomatic constructions? Correct the phrases that are not idiomatic.

1. The pressures of his or her job may cause the work-aholic to <u>get a nervous breakdown</u>.
2. <u>On a whole</u>, women seem more likely to report cases of sexual harrassment now.
3. The surgeon gestured frantically trying to <u>catch the nurse's eye</u>.
4. "<u>Be your age</u>," he snapped, not noticing the young boy's terror.
5. If <u>worst comes to worse</u>, evacuation of the island can <u>begin within twenty-four hours</u>.
6. The steering committee <u>agreed on</u> all aspects of the plan to circulate a petition.
7. The graphic artist <u>took pains</u> to make his preliminary sketches as complete as possible.
8. A set of weights and pulleys is likely to <u>come in handy</u> in the elementary-science classroom.
9. The mayor was completely <u>taken on</u> by the aide's suggestions.
10. Jogging is an <u>up and growing</u> pursuit in the United States today.

As you may have noticed in the previous exercise, preposition usage is also idiomatic. Certain prepositions are used with certain words as a matter of custom. In English this usage may once have been arbitrary, but it is now firmly fixed. We say a school "maintains a reputation *as* a fine institution," even though "maintains a reputation *of* a fine institution" gets the same point across. The unidiomatic statement just does **not ring true and makes the entire sentence seem awk-**ward. Although sometimes more than one preposition will sound right, usually there is only one acceptable pattern—and you need practice, not logic, to know what that pattern is. The easiest way to tell if you are using a preposition correctly is to consult a dictionary.

EXERCISE 5   Fill in the preposition that is idiomatic according to current English usage.

1. Her client felt it necessary to defend himself _____ the opposing counsel's accusations.
2. Martin Arrowsmith found personal satisfaction _____ helping people.
3. Oliver Twist's childhood was different _____ that of most other children.
4. _____ the course of his term as president, Hoover saw the nation slide into an economic depression.
5. Martin Luther King worked to bring about equality _____ peaceful means.
6. Elizabeth Blackwell had an early interest _____ the field of medicine.
7. Silas Lapham was always conscious _____ his position in the community.
8. Bertrand Russell did not have a belief _____ the ability of technology to solve all problems.
9. When preparing to debate, it helps if the participants have confidence _____ their own opinions.
10. Representational artists found it difficult to agree _____ the principles of Dada.

EXERCISE 6   Change the underlined prepositions to reflect idiomatic usage.

Many students become bored of school, and I'm no exception. So last semester I took some time off of school to see what working full time would be like. School was always pretty much of a drag for me. There just wasn't much to do. The strength of a school should be able to be measured on how many people hang around after classes are over. Here, no one does, and no wonder. You have a choice in whether to eat at the cafeteria or at a snack bar; you can go to the library, but most of the time I was discouraged of going because it's such a depressing place, and because my concentration was always being interrupted through noise. In class, it was no better. I hoped to do research <u>on</u> a field that interested me, but was stuck taking required survey courses, where the discussion always seemed to center <u>around</u> basics, and the instructors never took notice <u>to</u> my participation in class. Anyway, now, because of my experience <u>of</u> working in a neighborhood youth center, I am back in school majoring in social welfare. This time, it looks like I'll finish.

Levels of Usage

When you talk to a group of friends, you probably use some slang. All of us do. When you are talking to your employer or your instructor, you probably speak differently. The same is true in writing: a short note demands less formal language than a ten-page research paper. No one level of word usage is correct or incorrect. It is the situation that determines what type of language is appropriate or inappropriate.

1. Slang Slang expressions like "screwed up" or "ripped off" are most often used in speech. Though colorful and highly expressive, slang is too informal to be used in most writing, unless you are quoting someone or using it for some other special reason. To say that Beethoven's Ninth is "heavy" is like saying it is "great"—the word shows how you feel, but says little about the work. Then, too, slang will almost always clash in style with more formal subject matter. It sounds absurd to say:

After the lecture, the paleontologists decided to take off for the Museum of Natural History.

Finally, to describe a person as being "mean," "bad," "foxy," or "tough" is fine as long as your readers have an idea what you mean, but you cannot always be sure that your audience will be familiar with the slang expression you use.

2. Colloquial Style Like slang, colloquial style is mainly a way of speaking, and when used in writing it gives the impression of speech. Colloquial style is not as radical as slang; it sticks to the standard vocabulary of English. However, it is more relaxed and conversational than formal style. It uses contractions (*can't, don't, I've*) and shortened forms of words (*ad* for advertisement, *sub* for submarine), and often includes phrases that are not gramatically correct ("It's me" as opposed to "It is I").

Colloquial speech also uses "you" as a subject pronoun where more formal style would use "one."

Example: Colloquial: Making your own ice cream is an adventure.
              Formal: Making one's own ice cream is an adventure.

3. Formal Style Formal style is used on special occasions that call for dignity and seriousness. It does not use contractions, and it does not shy away from long words. In addition, it strives for absolute grammatical accuracy.

Formal diction can sound pretentious when it is used in the wrong situation, but when used at the right time, it can be effective. Religious leaders, politicians, and writers use this style when the occasion calls for it:

In order to appreciate Eliot's poetry, one must be acquainted with the work of the metaphysical poets.

We are gathered together to join these two people in holy matrimony.

Funerals, State of the Union addresses, and research papers would sound silly if they were laced with slang and colloquial phrases. So would informal essays and personal letters if they were clogged with large words and "impressive" phrases. Unfortunately, many people (politicians, for example) use long words whenever they can because they think it sounds more profound or more "educated." Instead of communicating simply and clearly they use unnecessarily formal diction. Whether accidentally or on purpose, they make a lot of noise with little meaning.

Some words seem overly formal in most circumstances. Notice the difference between the following pairs of words:

ill — sick	dine — eat
imbibe — drink	volume — book
repast — meal	purchase — buy
depart — leave	inebriated — drunk

4. Informal Style This style is best for much college writing. Tests and informal essays and reports can be written this way; however, research papers are usually more formal. Informal style is halfway between colloquial and formal English, and includes some qualities of each: it has the advantage of sounding something like speech, but having the grammatical precision of formal English. More and more, this level of diction is being used in serious writing. For example, it is used in this book.

EXERCISE 7

The following paragraph is informal, and the one that follows it is more formal. Compare the two paragraphs, commenting on shortened word forms, use of contractions, and other distinguishing characteristics of word choice you find. Notice also how the frequent use of the passive voice contributes to the second paragraph's more formal style.

As you grow older, you realize that you need some spending money. At age twelve you're too young to get working papers. You have to meet your expenses, so the only thing you can do is get a paper route. It starts off great, but after a while you begin to hate it. The job seems simple at first: you deliver papers to your customers. Then later you find out it's seven times a week at 6:30 every morning.

As one grows older, it becomes evident that some spending money is needed. A twelve-year-old is too young to get working papers, yet expenses must be met. One's only alternative is a newspaper route. It may begin well, but as time goes on, it no longer seems appealing. The job does not appear difficult: it merely consists of delivering newspapers to one's customers. Eventually, however, one discovers these deliveries must be made seven times a week at 6:30 every morning.

EXERCISE 8

Rewrite the following paragraph from a personal experience essay so that the style is more appropriate to the subject matter.

Once upon a time, back in the early spring of 1971, I chanced upon my first opportunity for gainful employment. This actually unpleasant experience forced me to gaze upon the janitorial industry with a scornful eye. In fact, the only thing that helped me to retain some measure of pride was the fact that the position I held was given the euphemistic title "Sanitation Engineer."

EXERCISE 9

Rewrite the following paragraph, an excerpt from a social welfare term paper on "Vagrancy in America," so that the style is more formal.

The American colonies were full of vagrants, men and women who didn't have jobs or places to live. Mostly, they were disobedient or runaway servants. The colonial settlement acts were supposed to get rid of the vagrant problem by keeping down travel. The laws said you needed a pass to move from one community to another, and you had to find a place to live for good right away. But in the long run, the settlement acts didn't get the results people wanted them to. This was mostly because the colonies needed a lot of workers who could move around freely and people didn't want to keep vagrants out of the labor force by making them stay in one place.

CHAPTER 13

Choosing the Right Word, Part II

When you write, you have many words from which to choose. Is the person you are trying to describe "crafty," "sneaky," or "stealthy"? Is the concept you want to define "general," "abstract," or "vague"? Finding the right word to express an idea may call for some thought, but it is worth the effort.

Choosing Specific Words

Vagueness of meaning can be caused by using generalizations in place of specific words and expressions. Whenever possible, choose a specific word or phrase instead of a general one.

General	Specific	Very Specific
book	novel	*Dune*
animal	ape	King Kong
writer	poet	William Carlos Williams
chemical	food additive	MSG

A specific term usually calls something definite to mind. On the other hand, general terms are often so vague that many times they are almost meaningless. For instance, look at the following statement:

Married couples should not have too many children.

This is a pretty broad generalization. At first, this sentence may appear to give you specific information, but when you examine it closely you find that it does not.

Does the writer mean *all* married couples? And how many children is "too many" anyway? Much more specific, and therefore more powerful in its impact, is the following:

> Married couples who feel strongly about the threat of overpopulation should not have more than two children.

You could add further detail: for instance, are you talking about couples in this country only? Does age (or health or religion) have anything to do with the decision to limit a family? Obviously, there are many more facts that could be provided. How much detail you include depends upon how much you need to make the point of your sentence clear.

Writing a critique of your freshman orientation program, you might first want to say:

> <u>Many people</u> felt the orientation program wasn't <u>long enough.</u>

But will this information really help the people organizing next year's orientation to avoid this year's mistakes? A slightly more helpful statement might be:

> <u>Many freshmen</u> felt the orientation program should have lasted <u>another day.</u>

"Many people" is vague; "many freshmen" is more concrete, but still does not have the effect that a more specific number or description would. "Should have lasted another day" is more specific than "wasn't long enough," but the question remains—what would the additional day have provided? Asking yourself such questions about your own writing can help you see how specific your words are. If you ask "what kind?" or "how many?" and your sentence gives no answer, you should probably use more specific language. Consider this statement:

Virtually all of the 300 out-of-state freshmen felt that another day of orientation would have given them a much needed opportunity to explore Boston before classes began.

Why say "some members of my family" when you can say "my father and I"? Why report "he shouted rude things at me" when you can tell what those things are? Why say only that you cut into the shark when your audience wants to know where you made the incision and how long it was?

EXERCISE 1

In the following pairs of sentences, show how changing vague words to specific ones changes meaning.

1. At times I have difficulty remembering what I have studied.
2. Before my exams I sometimes have difficulty remembering what I have studied.

1. Unemployment statistics indicate that minority groups are being hit hard by inflation.
2. Latest unemployment statistics show that minority groups have twice the unemployment of whites, and are therefore being hit hard by inflation.

1. Because of an experience in my past, I am terrified every time I ride in an automobile.
2. Because I was severely injured in an accident when I was ten, I am terrified every time I ride in an automobile.

EXERCISE 2

Read each of the sentences below, and fill in the blank with the first word that comes to your mind. These blanks represent the most important words in your sentence, because they carry the sentence's substance and meaning. Reread the completed sentence. If you find that these first thoughts are vague, abstract, overly familiar, and colorless—and surely some of them will be —rewrite each sentence, filling in the blanks with as many words as you need to make the sentence informative, accurate, and specific.

Example: The trouble with my wardrobe is _____.
The trouble with my wardrobe is that it's boring.
The trouble with my wardrobe is that it consists entirely of blue shirts, blue skirts, and blue jeans.

1. Our campus has a great many _____, but not many _____.

2. Freshmen may be described as _____, or perhaps as _____.

3. I certainly wouldn't characterize God as _____, but rather as ───────.

4. Whereas the preceding generation was _____, this generation is _____.

5. War is the most _____ ───────── I know.

6. Pollution is a _____ threat to our ───────.

7. Rock music is ───────, ───────, and ───────, but certainly not ───────.

8. When _____ died, I felt _____.

9. Men are _____, but women are ───────.

10. The sunset looked _____.

Choosing Original Words

A cliché is an expression that has lost much of its force through overuse. You may find yourself automatically using expressions such as "quick as a wink" or "good as gold" because they come so easily to mind. Unfortunately, because these phrases are so familiar, they make your writing seem flat. And if you state your case in expressions that everybody uses without thinking, your readers may suspect that you haven't been thinking very hard yourself.

Sometimes a cliché *can* be appropriate. This is especially true in conversation or even in colloquial writing when you wish to communicate an impression very quickly. Politicians, for instance, may use a cliché as "verbal shorthand"; it adds a touch of color without distracting their listeners from the subject. But in most writing, clichés add little to meaning and make a bad impression, and you need to find fresher, more vivid expressions.

If you walk out of an exam convinced you did extremely well, and want to let your friends know that, saying the questions were "as easy as pie" gets this point across. But reporting that the exam was "as easy as the midterm" will convey the level of the exam much more specifically, and have a lot more meaning to someone who knows how you felt about the midterm. A more concrete comparison can make your speech, or your writing, much clearer. And original comparisons can wake your writing up. "As familiar as an old shoe" may communicate adequately, but "as familiar as an old toothbrush" is less clichéd, and therefore more interesting and more meaningful.

EXERCISE 3

Rewrite the following clichés to substitute a word or phrase that is more specific, or more original, or both.

1. Damon stayed with Pythias <u>through thick and thin.</u>
2. Many of their contemporaries thought Sacco and Vanzetti were <u>wild-eyed radicals.</u>
3. Sherwood Anderson used the <u>sleepy village</u> of Winesburg, Ohio, as the setting for his novel.
4. In his autobiography *Born on the Fourth of July*, Vietnam veteran Ron Kovic describes himself as <u>American as Mom's apple pie.</u>
5. Small, fuel-efficient Japanese automobiles are <u>selling like hotcakes.</u>
6. A central theme of *The Godfather* is that <u>blood is thicker than water.</u>
7. In his classic short story "The Necklace," Guy de Maupassant shows that <u>honesty is the best policy.</u>
8. When Penelope saw her <u>long-lost</u> husband Odysseus, she turned <u>white as a sheet.</u>
9. Without his glasses, Stephen Dedalus was <u>blind as a bat.</u>
10. When Methuselah died, he was <u>as old as the hills.</u>

Choosing Effective Words

1. Connotation and Denotation   A word's *denotation* is what it means literally. Thus, "woman" and "lady" may denote exactly the same thing: an adult female. *Connotation*, however, involves feelings or impressions that a word brings to you—what the word suggests. "Woman" and "lady" have very different connotative meanings. To say that a female is a "woman" connotes maturity, self-respect, and self-reliance. To refer to the same person as a "lady" may suggest that she follows a definite code of proper behavior. The difference between the connotation and denotation of a word is a very important area of word meaning.

Consider the differences in connotation among the three words in each of the following sets. Although the words in each set denote the same thing, they clearly connote different things. How would you use each word?

smart	intelligent	brainy
frugal	thrifty	cheap
manly	macho	chauvinistic
obese	fat	chubby
confinement	imprisonment	rehabilitation
Mexican	Spanish-speaking	Chicano
pushy	ambitious	motivated
cautious	careful	timid
woman	mother	parent
untidy	disorderly	slob
black	colored	Negro

The situation in which a word is to be used is also very important. You would not refer to members of a feminist organization as "ladies" or "girls" but as "women," and if you were a psychiatrist you would not tell your patients they were "crazy."

EXERCISE 4

In each of the following blocks, list as many words or groups of words as you can that denote each underlined phrase. Then decide how each word or phrase might be appropriately used. In general, is the word appropriate for use in a letter to a friend, or on a term paper? In other cultures? In casual conversation? In formal situations?

Adult male: man,

Move on foot: walk,

Dwelling place: house,

Child: youth,

EXERCISE 5   Using the word lists you have just compiled, write ten sentences that are variations of the sentence:

> The adult male moved on foot into the dwelling place with the child.

Example: The <u>man</u> <u>walked</u> into the <u>house</u> with the <u>youth.</u>
The <u>letter carrier</u> <u>ran</u> into the <u>tent</u> with the <u>baby.</u>

You may add any adjectives or adverbs you like to make your sentences still more specific.

Example: The <u>old</u> man walked <u>quickly</u> into the house with the <u>frightened</u> youth.

1. The _____ _____ into the _____ with the _____.

2. The _____ _____ into the _____ with the _____.

3. The _____ _____ into the _____ with the _____.

4. The _____ _____ into the _____ with the _____.

5. The _____ _____ into the _____ with the _____.

6. The _____ _____ into the _____ with the _____.

7. The _____ _____ into the _____ with the _____.

8. The _____ _____ into the _____ with the _____.

9. The _____ _____ into the _____ with the _____.

10. The _____ _____ into the _____ with the _____.

In each of these sentences, the words you chose to fill in the blanks determined the meaning of your sentence, and gave it substance and purpose. Reread your sentences and make sure that the words you have used fit together, and have connotations that agree. "The young codger," for instance, sounds wrong; so does "the elderly guy."

EXERCISE 6

Choose one word or phrase within each set of brackets that says most accurately what you would like to say. When you have finished, go back over your paragraph and make certain your choices agree in connotation with each other.

The [car, automobile, limousine] approached [slowly, at a snail's pace, at moderate speed]. As it [passed by, whizzed by] my house, I could see [a young woman, a girl, a lady] sitting [alertly, tensely, stiffly] behind the wheel. I [realized, noticed, observed, discovered] she was wearing [glasses, eyeglasses, spectacles], and also that she had [golden, blonde, yellow, bleached] hair. [Suddenly, All at once, Startlingly], the car [halted, jerked to a stop, stopped]. The door opened, and the [young woman, girl, lady] got out. She [waited, stood idly by, stood still]; then she [drew, pulled, grabbed] something from her [handbag, purse, briefcase]. It was a [gun, pistol, Saturday night special, revolver]. I [closed, slammed down, shut] the window from which I had been [spying, looking, watching], and drew the [curtains, drapes, shade] closed.

EXERCISE 7

Discuss the differences in the connotations of the words in each of the following sets of words.

1. car
   automobile
   limousine

2. slowly
   at a snail's pace
   at moderate speed

3. young woman
   girl
   lady

4. alertly
   tensely
   stiffly

5. realized
   noticed
   observed
   discovered

6. glasses
   eyeglasses
   spectacles

7. golden
   blonde
   yellow
   bleached

8. Suddenly
   All at once
   Startlingly

9. halted
   jerked to a stop
   stopped

10. waited
    stood idly by
    stood still

11. drew
    pulled
    grabbed

12. handbag
    purse
    briefcase

13. gun
    pistol
    Saturday night special
    revolver

14. closed
    slammed down
    shut

15. spying
    looking
    watching

16. curtains
    drapes
    shade

In the following paragraph, an excerpt from a research
paper for a political science class, the words in each
bracketed group have similar meanings, but choosing
one over another may change the tone and meaning
of the paragraph. Discuss the differences in meaning
among the words in each group. Try to decide which
word in each group you might have chosen if you
had written the paragraph, paying special attention to
whether a word has a favorable, unfavorable, or neutral connotation; to avoiding repetition of words; and
to maintaining a style appropriate for a term paper.

The Tammany Society of New York, a political
organization, was formed in 1786, [borrowing, taking, lifting] its name from an Indian chief who was
said to have [welcomed, confronted, met] William
Penn. The [organization, group, club] also [adopted,
took, appropriated] Indian rites, ceremonials, and
titles of officials. [Nearly, Almost, Not quite] one
hundred years [later, after this, subsequent to this],
a [wave, flood, deluge] of immigration [gave, offered,
supplied, provided] strong support for the Tammany
Society. [In time, After a while, Eventually], the Society's [influence, clout, power] came to dominate
New York City politics. The candidates [pushed, supported, approved] by the "Wigwam" [seldom, hardly

ever, almost never] failed to win—[as a matter of fact, astonishingly, actually], Tammany support became [necessary, important, crucial] for victory.

2. Slanting As you have seen, choosing the right word can clarify your meaning. It can also *slant* it. *Slanted* words are not intended to be neutral. They have a connotation that is obviously positive or negative. For example, in the sentence "She expressed her feelings on the subject," the word "feelings" is neutral. In the sentence "She expressed her prejudices on the subject," however, the underlined word has a negative connotation. And in the sentence "She expressed her convictions on the subject," "convictions" has positive associations, because it suggests firm belief, well thought out.

Language can be slanted by including words or phrases or leaving them out. The statement "He was arrested for murder" is pretty damning; on the other hand, the inclusion of ". . . but released when it was discovered he had been having dinner with a friend at the time of the murder" changes the situation considerably. Substituting "with Officer Morris" for "with a friend" presents an even more favorable picture. Skillful use of slanted or "loaded" language, combined with careful inclusion and exclusion of informative words and phrases, can convey a very effective and subtle message. Slanting is used in campaign speeches, editorials, advertising copy, and even job applications, and can have its uses in your own essay writing as well.

EXERCISE 9

Rewrite the following sentences, taken from a positive review of a student production of *Hamlet*, so that the review will be negative. You may omit or add words, or simply substitute words with negative connotations for the positive words. However, do not replace words with others meaning the opposite (for example, "unconvincing" for "convincing").

1. Because of her facial expressions, the actress who played Gertrude was quite convincing in her role.

2. The sensitive portrayal of the melancholy Dane was particularly moving.
3. The stage sets were realistic.
4. The costumes were authentic and well made.
5. The dueling scene was very exciting.

Study the three paragraphs below, paying special attention to the underlined words. All three paragraphs describe an appearance made by a candidate for Congress. The first paragraph is an unbiased newspaper report.

> Jane Miller, Democratic/Liberal candidate for Congress from the 7th District, spoke at a <u>Daughters of the American Revolution</u> luncheon meeting today. Miller took a <u>firm</u> stand against <u>alleged</u> "reckless spending" by the federal government, citing its large allocations for nuclear weapons and spending in numerous other areas. Reading from a prepared text, Miller advanced a series of economic arguments against such spending. She was received politely by her largely <u>conservative</u> audience, who occasionally applauded.

Why does the above paragraph convey a neutral impression?

The second paragraph reads like a press release prepared by the candidate's supporters.

> Jane Miller, <u>popular</u> Democratic/Liberal candidate for Congress from the 7th District, spoke at a <u>political meeting</u> sponsored by the D.A.R. today. <u>Dr.</u> Miller took a <u>courageous</u> stand against government spending for <u>dangerous</u> and <u>unnecessary</u> stockpiling of nuclear weapons at the expense of needed social programs. Glancing only occasionally at her notes, Dr. Miller <u>forcefully</u> made a series of <u>provocative</u> points, winning unexpected smiles and nods of encouragement from her audi-

ence, who burst into <u>spontaneous</u> applause <u>again and again</u>.

How does the above paragraph use word choice and inclusion and exclusion of information to produce a favorable impression of Jane Miller?

The third paragraph might have been prepared by a particularly unscrupulous—and unsubtle—opponent.

> Jane Miller, <u>estranged wife</u> of John Miller of Grover's Point, took her <u>shoestring</u> campaign for Congress to a <u>ladies' luncheon</u> today. <u>Mrs.</u> Miller, wearing a navy blue dress and flowered hat, seemed nervous as she stood before the assembled ladies. Mrs. Miller's <u>questionable</u> stand against <u>necessary</u> government spending for the defense of our country's citizens was greeted with acts of <u>understandable</u> hostility from her <u>patriotic</u> audience. Reading <u>haltingly</u> from <u>crumpled</u> notes, the 40-year-old <u>sometime housewife and mother</u> tried <u>aggressively</u> to argue for her <u>impractical</u> economic policies.

How does the choice of language in the above paragraph create a negative impression of the candidate?

EXERCISE 11   Rewrite the following neutral account by altering word choice to create first a positive account and then a negative account of the same incident.

> William Leon, long-time Republican party spokesman, today addressed the American Association of Chicken Farmers in Great Bear, Indiana. Leon, dressed informally, told his audience that he, as a chicken farmer himself, could readily sympathize with their difficulties concerning federal price controls affecting agriculture. After the speech, Leon joined the group in a $100-a-plate chicken dinner.

CHAPTER 14

Revising
Your
Sentences and Words

As you can see by now, revision of an essay involves several steps. First, you examine your essay's over-all structure. Second, you check the individual paragraphs of your essay and make sure that they are well constructed and perform the functions they are supposed to. Finally, you carefully read your work as a whole, paying careful attention to sentence structure and word choice.

The student who submitted the following paper had little trouble with organization and paragraph structure. Her sentence structure and word choice, however, caused problems for her. Her instructor suggested that she consider the following points when revising her essay:

Sentences and Words

Are your sentence patterns correct?
  Are there sentence fragments?
  Are there run-on sentences?
  Are modifiers in the proper places?
  Are elements in a series parallel?
  Are there uncalled-for shifts in subject, voice, number, person, or mood?
  Have you varied your sentence patterns?
  Do you overuse certain words?
  Are your words exact enough?
  Do you always use your words or expressions correctly?
  Are there inappropriate shifts in diction levels?
  Is your style appropriate to your subject?

Do your words have the connotations you want
them to have?
Are you sure you know the meanings of all the
words you use?

Comments   **Rough Draft**

My Freshman English Course

*Who was going to
college?*

[Going to college,] my English skills were pretty
good. I thought that I would have no trouble at all with

Diction level

English. [Boy, was I surprised!] My first [English

*Repetition—you
overuse "English
course."*

course] gave me lots of trouble. My first [English course]
was freshman composition. This class was chiefly con-

Idiom?

cerned with writing [single typed paged papers.] The
topics of these papers varied. Sometimes we were free
to choose our topics, but usually we were assigned a
specific [thought *word?*] to [write on. *preposition?*] The [given *word?*] topics

Subject shift

were [based on how we viewed *redundant* situations or how you
cope with certain situations.]

We were also urged to write [other extra] papers
on [self chosen *idiom?*] topics. At the [end of the term,] we

Redundant

could pick any of the term papers and hand them in
for a [final term's] grade. I wrote on a short story by
James Joyce called "Araby." I thought I had done a

*A word like
"however" can't
be used as a
coordinating
conjunction.
Comma splice*

good job, [however,] when I got the paper back, I
found that I had made many mistakes.   *diction level*

The textbook we used in our course was [o.k.] We
were assigned chapters to read, and would discuss them
the following class period. Sometimes we would read
excerpts from [known *idiom?* authors'] works and discuss

Parallel series

them too. [The works we read illustrated narrative,
descriptive, and also we examined expository forms of
writing.]

Excess phrase

[Although I would much rather read than write,] I found my first college English course bearable. I found myself [somewhat] [non-motivated] but I stuck it

Run-on sentence

out. [When it came to writing that is.] [Perhaps this semester I will have it easier the course I have now concentrates on reading.]

You express yourself honestly and include a fair amount of detail; paragraphing is logical and your controlling idea is clear. Still, this essay has a number of errors in sentence structure and word usage. Try a revision.

Comments

Revision 1

My Freshman English Course

Better, but choppy sentences. Try to combine some of these. Also use transitions.

When I went to college, I felt my English skills were pretty good. I thought that I would have no trouble at all with this subject. I certainly was surprised. My first English course gave me lots of trouble.

Still not idiomatic

In freshman English, we were chiefly concerned with writing [single spaced typed one paged papers.] The topics of these papers varied. Sometimes we were free to choose our topics, but usually we were assigned

This sentence could be smoother— eliminate double "situations."

a specific one to discuss. Many times these topics were based on how we viewed situations or how we coped with certain situations.

Throughout the following two paragraphs you use very few details. Can you try to make these paragraphs more vivid?

We were also urged to write extra papers about topics we chose ourselves. At the end of the term we could pick any one of these papers and hand them in for a grade. I wrote about a short story I read by James Joyce called "Araby." I thought I had done a good job; however, when I got my paper back, I found that I had made many mistakes.

Inexact usage

The textbook we used in our course was [all right.] We were assigned chapters to read, and would discuss them the following class period. Sometimes we would

Repetition

read excerpts from the [works] of well-known authors and discuss them too. The [works] we read illustrated narrative, descriptive, and expository forms of writing.

I found my first college English course bearable. Al-

Choppy conclusion Also very general. Can you make it more specific?

though I was unmotivated, I stuck it out. When it came to writing, I just was not interested. Perhaps this semester I will have it easier because the course I have now concentrates on reading.

> *You've done a good job of correcting the errors I pointed out on your last draft—sentence structure and word choice are much improved. Now work on your style to eliminate generalizations and repetition, and to add smoother transitions between your somewhat choppy sentences. And now comes the hard part: see if more effective use of detail and a more imaginative introduction and conclusion can add some life to the essay; try varying sentence patterns and using more vivid and concrete words.*

Comments

Revision 2

My Freshman English Course

Before I went to college, I felt that my English skills

Much more concrete

were good. I thought that I would have no [trouble at all writing essays or term reports.] My first English course, however, proved how mistaken I was.

In freshman English, we were primarily concerned

More specific

with [writing four-hundred-word essays.] Sometimes we were assigned specific topics, and other times we could write about anything at all. It was when we were given freedom to choose our own topic that I had the most trouble. I never could think of a thing to write. If

I had been better at English, I might have said I had "writer's block."

Our teacher urged us to write extra papers based on independent reading. At the end of the term, she asked us to pick our best paper and submit it for a grade. The paper I handed in was about my impressions of a short story I had read by James Joyce called "Araby." When I got my paper back and saw how many errors there were, I felt [as disillusioned as the boy in the story.]

Good analogy

The textbook we used was [satisfactory but not very stimulating.] We were assigned chapters to read and would discuss them in class. Most of us were not particularly interested in talking about writing as much as we did. The best part of the class was when we read excerpts from the works of well-known writers. These selections did a lot to help me understand narrative, descriptive, and expository forms of writing.

Better

Even though freshman English hurt my ego, I did stick it out. In spite of myself I think I even learned something about writing. Next semester I am going to take an English course that concentrates on reading. Perhaps then, when I am asked to write, I will find that all my suffering has paid off.

EXERCISE

What changes did the writer make between her second and third drafts? Would you have made the same changes? What other changes were possible?

Appendix

A Combined Checklist

Organization   Does your essay have:
- An introduction?
- A body?
- A conclusion?
- A controlling idea?
- Topic sentences?
- A restatement of the controlling idea in the conclusion?

The Paragraphs   Does your introduction:
- Arouse interest?
- Adequately introduce the subject?
- Smoothly lead to the controlling idea?

Do your body paragraphs:
- Have topic sentences?
- Provide focus?
- Have supporting details?
- Include adequate transitions?

Does your conclusion:
- Restate the controlling idea?
- Contain general concluding remarks?
- Have a final closing statement?

Sentences and Words   Are your sentence patterns correct?
- Are there sentence fragments?
- Are there run-on sentences?
- Are modifiers in the proper places?
- Are elements in a series parallel?
- Are there uncalled-for shifts in subject, voice, number, person, or mood?
- Have you cut out deadwood and redundancy?
- Have you varied your sentence patterns?
- Do you overuse certain words?
- Are your words exact enough?
- Do you always use your words or expressions correctly?
- Are there inappropriate shifts in diction levels?

241

Index

Agreement, 194–200
  pronoun-antecedent, 197–200
  subject-verb, 194–197

Body paragraphs, essay, 6, 96–121
  development of, 106–110
Brainstorming, 30–33

Comma splices, 176–177
Concluding paragraph, essay, 7, 122–137
  chronological wind-up in, 126–127, 135
  course of action recommended in, 130–131
  illustration in, 127–128, 136
  prediction in, 128–130
  quotation or dialogue in, 131–132, 135
  restatement in, 125–126, 134
Conjunction, coordinating, 150
Connotation, 227–228
Controlling idea, essay, 5, 34–39, 40–48, 74–75, 96–97, 123
  broad, 35–39, 44–48, 74
  narrow, 34–35, 36–39, 40–44, 74

Deadwood in sentences, 160–161
Denotation, 227–228

Economy in sentences, 160–166
Essay
  general structure of, 3–5, 8–9
  revision of, 65–69
  three-point, 6

Idioms, 214–217

Introductory paragraph, essay, 5–6, 73–95
  anecdote in, 79–81
  definition in, 81–82, 91–92
  direct announcement in, 76–78, 89, 93
  question in, 86–87, 91
  quotation or dialogue in, 78–79, 92
  refutation in, 82–84
  unrelated facts in, 84–86, 91

Listing, 29–30

Modifiers
  in simple sentence, 146–147
  dangling, 185–186
  misplaced, 182–185

Parallelism, 186
  faulty, 186–191
Perspectives, shifting, 191–194
  in number, 191–192
  in person, 192
  from statement to question, 192
  in tense, 191
  in voice, 191
Predicate, 145–146

Redundancy, 161–166
Revision, 65–69, 138–141, 236–240
  essay, 65–69
  paragraphs, 138–141
  sentence, 236–240
  word, 236–240

Sentence patterns, 145–159, 173–176
  complex, 151–153, 154–155, 158–159
  compound, 150–151, 154–155, 157–158

compound-complex, 154
  fragment, 173–176
  fused, 176–177
  run-on, 176–181
  simple, 145–149, 156
Sentence variety, 166–172
Structuring patterns, 56–62
  cause and effect, 59–60
  classification and division, 60–61
  comparison—contrast, 57–59
  illustration, 56–57
  process, 61–62
Style
  colloquial, 218
  formal, 218–219
  informal, 219
  slang, 217
Subject, simple sentence, 145–146

Topic, essay, 24–33
  angled, 24–26
  boundaries of, 26–28
  general, 25
  limited, 24–26
Topic sentence, 6, 96–106
  placement of, 100–106
Transition, 110–113

Usage, levels of, 217–221

Words
  commonly confused pairs, 207–214
  effective, choice of, 227–235
  inexact usage of, 205–207
  original, choice of, 225–226
  overused, 203–205
  slanting of, 233–235
  specific, choice of, 222–225